BE BRAVE. LOSE THE BEIGE!

Finding Your Sass After Sixty

LIZ KITCHENS

SHE WRITES PRESS

Published 2023
Printed in the United States of America
Print ISBN: 978-1-64742-468-8
E-ISBN: 978-1-64742-469-5
Library of Congress Control Number: 2022914822

For information, address:
She Writes Press
1569 Solano Ave #546
Berkeley, CA 94707

Interior Design by Tabitha Lahr

She Writes Press is a division of SparkPoint Studio, LLC.

This book is dedicated to my husband Jim. His belief in me is the scaffolding that supports my dreams and aspirations.

Contents

INTRODUCTION:

An Ode to Beige

Meet the motto of *Be Brave. Lose the Beige!*:

> Running from appointment to appointment, checking off a to-do list—that isn't really living. Discovering the playful side of life. Spreading joy. Skirting a few rules. Being colorful . . . clever . . . creative. Now *that's* living.

Society has decidedly beige expectations, particularly when it comes to aging. *Be Brave. Lose the Beige!* pokes fun at these societal rules and expectations and encourages you to discover your colorful spirit in this aging adventure into the wonderland of your sixty-plus-year-old self.

Meet Beige. Beige is reliable, practical, sensible, and safe. Beige doesn't put up a fuss; it is very accommodating and goes with everything. Beige is conflict averse, follows the rules, blends in, and avoids standing out. Now meet Magenta. Magenta and her sister jewel tones are rich, dynamic, loud, sometimes garish, and not easily overlooked. Magenta doesn't always mix well with others. Magenta is hard to ignore.

Beige is endorsed—even encouraged—by our society. Governing bodies prefer their citizens in beige. Too many screaming magentas and shrieking yellows, and there's trouble in River City. Or so we're told. But maybe some rebellion is warranted at this stage in our lives. The biggest danger intrinsic to being beige is that it precludes creative thinking. Armed with a beige brush, our purses and sofas aren't the only items we color vanilla. We also tend to beige up our choices, goals, and life strategies.

I'm not quite as beige-phobic as I may sound. I have a beige sofa, beige clothing, and beige purses. But speaking more existentially, more universally, beige represents the antithesis of creative living. As an avowed creativity evangelist, I know creative thinking is critical to navigating what's next for baby boomers.

Baby boomer women, Lady Boomers as I like to call us (I was born in 1953 and most assuredly fit this demographic), have lived a significant portion of our adult years within very prescribed lines. Our kindergarten teachers' admonishment to "color inside the lines" has guided many of our life choices. Our lives have been a linear sequence of education, work, babies, minivans, college tuition, parental caretaking, and grandparenting. Little if any of our time has been designated to pursue our own passions. We've worn and continue to wear a lot of hats—as professionals, mothers, volunteers, wives, daughters, and Grandmothers (with a capital G because, of course, grandparenting is God's reward for having produced children). Multitasking these roles, however, can lead to multi-taxing our spirits. This contributes to beige-dom: beige choices and beige goals. And, as I think we're all painfully aware, our society has decidedly beige expectations about aging. But don't forget who we are! Though we're in our sixties and seventies (some of us even knocking hard on the door to eighty), we're the kids of the psychedelic '60s. We tuned in, turned on, and took over! "Flower Power" was a slogan of resistance to the Vietnam War, and I say it's time we resurrect that brilliant icon, a veritable palette of vibrant colors, as a symbol of resistance in the war on aging. Hippies were members of a 1960's countercultural youth movement that rejected the mores of mainstream American life, so it's kind of ironic that many of us are having our arthritic hips surgically replaced. But let's use those new hips (and old ones) to march against the culture of ageist notions.

Our earlier life stages came with guidebooks and mentors to help us navigate dating, marriage, and the pitfalls of parenting. But where are the practical resources to help us navigate the issues we face as we age? The examples set by our parents, many of them now long gone, don't necessarily work for our generation. We're far more active, living longer, and may not have the financial resources to afford the leisurely retirements that our parents' generation enjoyed.

And what about the words and phrases that define this stage in our lives? I've been singularly underwhelmed by the labels people have concocted to describe our post middle-age years. I have heard references to The Vintage Years (hate it); Act 3 or Chapter 3 (not a fan); The Afternoon of Our Lives (nah). "I'm on my Next to the Last Dog," a euphemism coined by Marc Freedman of Encore.org, is funny but cumbersome.

Lady Boomers: I propose BBLB—Be Brave. Lose the Beige!—as the moniker for this moment in our lives. BBLB is sassy and pokes fun at societal rules and norms. It says yes when the world says no. Let's start a new trend and call our post-middle age years our BBLB years. As you contemplate what's next for you, I'm hoping the stories and fun exercises in this interactive book will inspire you to think creatively about your own future. Perhaps that even means playing with the concept of a self-designed retirement. Given our financial fears, we might need to consider blurring the lines between work and leisure, redefining the traditional ideas about the very nature of retirement.

Be Brave. Lose the Beige began as a blog and evolved into stories that chronicle how creative thinking helped this baby boomer cope with Empty Nest Syndrome, navigate sex over sixty, and transition from being outtasight to being *literally* out of sight. Exercising your creativity promotes creative thinking, which is essential in navigating your BBLB years, so the conclusion of each of these chapters features creative exercises designed to help you trot out your inner Magenta and color outside the lines.

I'm a numbers junkie. One hat I wear is that of pollster, and as such I've collected data on a variety of Lady Boomer issues, including, but not limited to, our fashion choices, our propensity for people pleasing, and our personality characteristics. For example, eighty percent of baby boomer women describe themselves as reliable and dependable (versus spontaneous and flexible—27% or creative—28%). Seriously?! "Reliable and dependable" are the dominant personality traits we use to define ourselves? Of course, dependability and reliability are perfectly wonderful qualities in a partner, parent, or friend. But don't we want a *little* more for ourselves? These words describe someone in service to others, which is admirable, of course, but a far cry from sassy. Yes, we derive joy from caring for our families and friends. But it's easy to lose pieces of ourselves if we spend too much time in service to others.

The first baby boomers began turning sixty-five in 2011. This group is 79 million strong, and 51 percent of us are women. Rumor has it that over half the baby boomers in America are going to celebrate our one hundredth birthdays and beyond. But today's longevity presents a whole host of issues that need attention. Contending with formerly functioning body parts and figuring out our financial futures are chief among them. Also, many of us continue to be 911 on our adult children's cell phones. Even as they crest toward forty-plus, we're still on call to help manage their anxieties, offer advice, and, all too often, clean up their monetary messes. But ladies, we're not getting any younger, so let's stop postponing ourselves and start coloring outside some lines.

For easy reference, *The BBLB Manual of Maxims* can be found on page 216. Feel free to refer to this handbook or even develop your own maxims, defining what constitutes acceptable rule breaking for you. Deciding what's best for you is part of your creative journey. (I realize the irony in creating a rule book for rule breaking, but I'm a sucker for a good irony.)

CHAPTER 1:

The Creativity Evangelist

*"Every child is an artist. The problem is
how to remain an artist once he grows up."*
—PICASSO

"You think rules are just suggestions!" friends and family
members have accused.

"Not true," replies my pollster self. "I just think some
of them have a margin of error." I want to rebrand the
term, "rule-breaking" and call it "creative thinking." A
key to avoiding a beige life is thinking creatively, even if
a few pesky rules get trampled in the process.

The term "creativity" can be intimidating and often
misunderstood. Sadly, I've known far too many people who
have been saddled with the label "not creative" since their
earliest years. I've proposed creative projects, then watched
grown women dart from the room declaring, "Oh, no I'm
not creative at all." That reaction hurts my heart because
I believe there is a creative outlet for everyone, one that
doesn't necessarily involve picking up a paintbrush and
standing before an easel. Trying a new recipe is creative.
Getting dressed in the morning can be a creative act.
Rearranging furniture is a creative act. Most important,

creativity is a way of thinking about and approaching many aspects of your life, and it makes an excellent partner in our BBLB years. Aging isn't necessarily fun, but our later years can certainly be full of fun. Creativity cultivates fun. And it offers buoyancy to hearts often laden with worry.

I am an avowed creativity evangelist on a crusade to spread the word about the potential life-changing capabilities of creativity. Writer Laura Holson's 2015 *New York Times* article entitled, "We're All Artists Now" validates this contention. Holson writes,

> *Our best selves are merely one doodle away. Where once drawing and other painterly pursuits were the province of starving artists or simply child's play, unlocking one's creativity has become the latest mantra of personal growth and healing.*[1]

The article notes that creativity has the same holistic benefits as a weekend at the Canyon Ranch Resort and Spa (and costs a lot less, I might add). In that vein, the Mayo Clinic recommends the health benefits of painting and ceramics. A four-year study cited in the online magazine *Better Aging* found that people who took up creative endeavors in middle age suffered less memory loss.[2]

Author Elizabeth Gilbert, of *Eat, Pray, Love* fame, wrote in her later book, *Big Magic,* that creativity isn't about dropping everything and becoming an opera star but rather about living a life driven more strongly by curiosity than fear.[3]

COVID CREATIVITY

As I wrote this book, Covid was plaguing our planet. And didn't we all witness (and exhibit) a whole lot of creativity in reaction to the pandemic? In a flash, fear of infection led to creative thinking. Shuttered cafés began offering deliveries and curbside pickup of menu items, including booze-filled beverages. Gallon jugs of sangria and happy hour old fashioneds were a welcome relief for people sheltering in place. As people struggled to manage fear and anxiety, religious organizations responded by streaming worship services, daily meditations, and Zoom Sunday school classes. Tech-savvy curators helped people access museums by offering virtual tours of their collections. With fitness centers closed, the quarantine fifteen crept into living rooms when we weren't looking (were we busy baking bread?), so cyclists punched their credit card numbers into Peloton's website; yoga gurus conducted Zoom sessions and outdoor classes; and more than a few garages were converted to home gyms. People didn't give up; they made Darwin proud by adapting.

Western societies often marginalize creativity. It gets patted on the head and told to stay in its place. When school budgets dwindle, the arts are the first to go. During Covid's early stages, however, it was the creative thinkers and entrepreneurs who recognized that the economic distress was almost as contagious as the virus. They looked for opportunities as they scrambled to put their Humpty Dumpty finances back together again. Many not only survived the crisis but thrived.

My crusade extols the virtues of creativity and creative thinking as a means of enhancing our quality of life and helping us survive economic downturns. And how about this for an argument in favor of a more creative life: A 2019 National Institute of Health Study found that creative engagement by older adults results in fewer doctors' visits, less dependence on medication, fewer falls, memory enhancement, and a sense of belonging.[4]

What if you're intrigued by this idea of creative thinking as a way to arrest aging but don't view yourself as creative? How do you rip off that bulky "uncreative" label and cultivate this quality? It calls for some exercise.

BBLB Manual of Maxims #1:
"Exercise your creative muscles."

EXERCISE YOUR CREATIVITY

We all recognize the benefits of physical exercise. Weight training, biking, skiing, and swimming most certainly contribute to good health and well-being. Exercising our minds has similar benefits. We've all taken classes, read novels and news magazines, and solved crossword puzzles and other brain games in the interest of keeping our noggins nimble. But once we transition from our teens, we tend to spend less and less time on creative endeavors. And just like physical muscles that fail to be engaged, so too can our creative muscles atrophy.

A 2019 *Forbes Magazine* article asked, "Can We Train Our Creative Muscles?" The response? A resounding yes!

> *Creativity can be trained, and through practice, our creative muscles can improve their flexibility. One sure-fire way to boost creative thinking? Try. Creativity is, in fact, a skill—not a gift—that can be learned and mastered at any age.[5]*

Albert Einstein was quoted as saying, "Genius is 1% talent and 99% hard work." I think something similar can be said for creativity. I'd go with ten percent natural talent and ninety percent hard work, the practicing and polishing of our skills.

IS IT TOO LATE TO START?

Jeffrey Kluger, in his 2013 *Time Magazine* article, "How to Live Long" contends that creativity *increases* with age. He writes,

> *Studies have found the brain continues to grow in those areas involving creativity. The very deterioration we dread actually enhances creativity. The walls break down. It's no longer language in the left hemisphere and art in the right. There is a free flow of information back and forth.*[6]

Maybe this is why Grandma Moses, Pablo Picasso, Georgia O'Keeffe, and Judy Chicago did some of their best work later in life.

Since 2003, I have been the director of a creative expression program for at-risk teens. The first thing I observe in these classes is that the arts (in my case, ceramics) offer a refuge, even an oasis, for kids whose lives are fraught with turmoil and hardship. For two hours, time is suspended as each step in the development of a clay dragon or cereal bowl informs the next. That's the creative process in a nutshell: one step informing the next. And that's how we should address aging issues, each step informing us what to do next.

I propose that creative fitness become a public health issue. The President's Council on Sports, Fitness, and Nutrition already exists, and it's time we create a similar program for creative fitness. Until relatively recently, creativity has been the Rodney Dangerfield of public health, but it's time to give creativity the respect it deserves.

LIGHTING THE FUSE

It's now been thirty years since I first took the advice I'm espousing here. When I was thirty-seven and newly ensconced in a second marriage, I enrolled in a pottery class. Perhaps it was finding "the one" that freed me from having to spend time looking for love and allowed me to focus on creative endeavors. Or maybe it was the fact my mother was no longer alive. My mother had been intensely creative. No room in my tiny, three-bedroom childhood home was off limits to her creative wand. Rummage sales and thrift stores supplied her decorating palate with eclectic pieces, including an old upright piano she refinished and played. I arrived home one afternoon from high school to find her sitting in a vintage rattan peacock chair she had unearthed at a church thrift store and repainted. Mom was also a writer who authored books on astrology. In retrospect, I can see that creativity was her refuge, providing comfort from the pain and disappointment of her failing marriage. But as a teen girl, all I knew was that there was simply no psychic or even architectural space for me to compete. So, I postponed that part of myself, afraid I might not measure up.

With fear of maternal judgment no longer a factor after my mother died, a friend and I enrolled in a beginner's pottery class at a local art center. The Maitland Art Center was conceived as an artist colony in the 1930s by visionary artist and architect, Andre Smith. The center's Mayan-influenced architecture and artistic atmosphere provided a welcoming environment in which to explore and re-ignite my long dormant creative fuse, and I began to thrive there. My friend quit after the fourth session, but I signed on for life.

I WOEFULLY UNDERESTIMATED the power and seduction of the clay, and its capacity to ground and center me. According to M.C. Richards, author of a seminal book on pottery, *Centering*, "Clay comes from the ground and grounds those who touch it."[7] Centering a piece of clay on a spinning wheel is difficult (understatement). But somehow, wrapping my wobbling hands around a lump of clay was indeed grounding, and the centering process became a metaphor for centering my own life. Clay proved to be a perfect medium to fit my nature because pottery doesn't require the precision of a medium such as pen/pencil drawing. Thank goodness, as precision is hardly a predominant characteristic of mine. Right away, I loved the flexible, forgiving nature of the clay. Clay has also taught me life lessons. When throwing on the wheel, the potter strives to balance being firm with being gentle and knowing when to fight vs. when to surrender as the clay struggles to fly off the wheel head.

Art therapists tell us there is a spectrum of art materials. This spectrum ranges from mediums that offer precision to those that thrive in chaos. Pen and pencil are the most controlled of the art materials; finger-paints are the least. Clay is on the looser end of the continuum and exploring that end of the artistic spectrum gave me permission to not be so hard on myself about my lack of sketching skills.

The art of pottery also juxtaposes aesthetics and func-tionality. People have been creating pottery for centuries, and for many cultures pottery was essential for cooking, serving, and storing food. To this day, it still serves those functions but also maintains its identity as an object of art and an avenue for artistic expression. The functionality and practicality of the craft attracted me immediately. "I'll be able to create dinner dishes for my family and vases for gifts all while playing in clay!" I marveled.

I've concluded that Lady Boomers tend to justify the time they spend on self-enriching endeavors, and that thought was most definitely in the back of my mind when I signed up for the class. What a cost savings, I calculated. (Of course, as is the case with most hobbies, my pottery habit ended up costing me thousands. Savings from creating my own dinnerware and gifts? Negligible.)

Becoming a potter not only gave me artistic joy and gifts to share, but the pursuit also expanded the way I think. I began to think more creatively about the surveys I designed for my market research firm. This enriched way of thinking made me more willing to take risks. I conceived and developed a pottery program for under-served youth. When I turned fifty-five, I started writing a blog. So, because I've exercised one set of creative muscles, others have strengthened as well. And my hope is that by exercising your own creative muscles your thinking will expand as you navigate your BBLB years.

BREAKING THE RULES AT SEVENTY

For months preceding my husband's seventieth birthday, I begged him to allow friends and family to celebrate this milestone occasion. I proposed a catered dinner for family and friends or a pilgrimage to his native Atlanta, kind of a "best of Jim Kitchens" tour. His son suggested a family golf tournament at Calloway Gardens, complete with brunch and cocktail party. My son lobbied for an island paradise retreat at Sanibel Island for kids and grandchildren. Bloated credit cards and family fights, however, didn't sound like paradise to Jim.

"Well, what do *you* want?" I finally asked.

"I want to go someplace beautiful with you, someplace we've never been, someplace where I can unplug and be wasted for five days."

That's when I realized how saddled my almost-seventy-year-old husband had been with too many obligations and responsibilities. He had recently extracted himself from a side business that for too long had required him to exercise management skills he didn't really have. He wanted a getaway that really felt like a break. Southern California beckoned as a good short-term destination site for our trip with the added bonus of legal marijuana edibles. "That will certainly help you unplug," I offered. My hippie husband didn't hesitate to say yes.

Travel as a twosome had become increasingly rare for us. Our "away time" was usually devoted to kids and grandchildren living in other cities. So we planned and then savored the anticipation of our romantic getaway, just as we'd done in our younger years.

Which brings me to 4:00 a.m., Eastern Time on our departure date. Our 6:30 a.m. flight meant getting up excruciatingly early, the upside being that we'd arrive in California at 8:30 a.m. Pacific Time with an entire day of 68-degree sunny weather beckoning. Our early-to-bed strategy, however, precluded us from seeing the midnight message from Southwest Airlines advising us that our flight had been cancelled. Instead, we saw the text the next morning, *after* our showers and coffee injections.

The customer service lady unlucky enough to be answering calls at 4:45 in the morning told us, "That was the only nonstop flight today. The only other flight we can get you on leaves at 6:00 p.m. going through Kansas City and getting into San Diego at 10 p.m. And given this late booking, you'll be boarding in group C. But don't you worry, your early bird fees for your previously booked flight will be refunded back to your credit card."

Crushed, we went back to bed and pulled the covers over our heads.

Four hours of nightmare-infused sleep later, we set about contacting Hertz, the Hotel Del, and Southwest for more begging and pleading. Once again, we were reminded we would be in the last boarding group, which all but guaranteed that we'd be stuck in middle seats back by the restrooms, with little to no overhead bin space for our bags. "That is, unless you're eligible for pre-boarding," the new rep added, seemingly as an afterthought.

Pre-boarding? Ding ding ding! I suddenly pictured myself in a line full of people in wheelchairs, queued up for early admission to the plane. I decided my impending knee replacement surgery for my damaged right knee qualified me for pre-boarding. So, donning a knee brace, I was ready for my disability début.

BBLB Manual of Maxims #2:
"It's easier to ask for forgiveness than permission."

Caveat: Once you start down the rule-breaking road it may be hard to stop. I decided a cane would add pageantry to my airport presentation, so I found a medical supply store en route to the airport. And since I'd be in the store anyway (and because I tend to be a productivity-a-holic), I could make arrangements for medical equipment to be delivered to my house for my post knee replacement convalescence in three weeks.

So onward we drove to the airport for our evening flight. All things considered, Orlando International Airport is a great airport. Lots of restaurants and shops, and all the Disney World, Universal, and SeaWorld paraphernalia you could want awaits you for mere hundreds of dollars. They also have extensive parking. Except on that day. Barreling into and intending to go upward in the winding garage we were halted by a parking attendant attired in his fluorescent yellow safety vest. "The garages are completely full. You'll have to park somewhere else." One by one, cars exited per instruction. All except one. Ours. "We were planning to valet park at the Hyatt. Can we still do that?" my husband asked. "Sure, no problem," the attendant said, moving the barricade aside. Full confession: we had no intention of valet parking for four days at premium prices. As a seasoned air traveler, my husband didn't believe there were no spots to be had. And his suspicions were confirmed. We counted at least ten self-parking spaces on the first floor alone. Our chicanery was paying off. Do real con artists experience this kind of adrenaline rush?

Southwest was more than happy to share their inventory of wheelchairs with me. I flopped my somewhat disabled self into one and cued up in a line of ten awaiting porters to usher us through to the gate. And we waited and waited.

"Can my husband take me?" I tentatively asked.

"Sure!" the Southwest employee replied, looking quite happy to be relieved of one of her burdens. So away we sailed to the security line, dragging our rolling bags along like rotund, obedient pets and trying to avoid careening into innocent bystanders.

"You're so slow!" I admonished my husband/driver. "This chair won't go," he defended. "There's too much stuff on here."

"Did you just call me 'stuff'?" I jabbed.

"Oh wait," said Jim, "the brake is on. Now that's better." Sympathetic people seemed to take pity on us, even offering assistance in lieu of being harpooned by my cane.

Jim finished pushing me to the Southwest gate area and zipped over to the agent to see what he could do to put our derailed getaway back on track. I hung back, piled high with backpacks, sandwiches, and luggage. Moments later, my husband appeared disco dancing down the corridor waving new boarding passes. For $50, we moved from group C to group A! "No contending with middle seats and stinky bathrooms," we rejoiced. Within seconds, the wheelchair was parked and off came the knee brace as we aborted our pre-boarding plan. I actually had mixed feelings, but the pseudo faking-it thing was already growing old.

Talking with my son earlier in the day, I expressed my disappointment over losing an entire day out of the five we had scheduled for our vacation getaway. But rather than allowing me to whine like a spoiled child, my psychologist son said, "I spend a lot of my practice counseling people on managing disappointments. How a person handles disappointment can be transformative."

That counsel stayed with me, helping me transform our disappointment at the flight delay into a mini adventure. The fact is our sneaky stunts set the tone for the rest of our trip. It started us off with a spirit of defiance and adventure. It was fun being rule breakers at 66 and 70. #ifnotnowwhen?

Breaking little rules can feel empowering, and my inner renegade had no problem "sticking it to the man," in this case Southwest Airlines and Orlando International Airport. We asserted some personal control in a situation that made us feel there was little control to be had. Questioning and pushing back—even a little—in situations that make us feel powerless is empowering and the very definition of coloring outside the lines. That said, while breaking little rules offers a sense of control, don't do it at the expense of others. Jim and I made ourselves feel better about our little stunts by not asking a porter to wheel me through security, and we returned the wheelchair to its designated space. We also eased our potential parking guilt by making sure there were plenty of self-parking spaces available in that garage we slipped our way into. Nothing wrong with a little polishing, even when one is being a rebel.

BBLB Manual of Maxims #3:
"Breaking little rules is empowering." (Just don't do it at the expense of others.)

THE THREE-FISTED DRINKER

Breaking rules is different from breaking laws. I think most of us have lived a good portion of our lives within the confines of one authority or another, and we learned a whole lot of rules. Our parents told us what to do and how to behave; teachers and principals held us to a code of conduct; employers dictate our days, and even our children and grandchildren seem bent on saddling us with rules ("No, mom, *that's* not how you play the game!"). We tend to internalize these behavioral edicts and regard them as seriously as laws we're expected to follow.

As we move through our BBLB years, let us decide which behavioral rules work for us and which don't. Taking small steps that break with convention nourishes the quality of our days. One such tiny break with convention I employ is my three-drink strategy.

Growing up I was allowed one drink per meal. Milk or orange juice for breakfast, iced tea for dinner. I suspect that as a child I chafed at these constraints because as an adult I can't resist ordering multiple beverages. A glass of wine offers a little buzz that I enjoy, the caffeine from my iced tea keeps me awake and alert, and ice water quenches my thirst. This liquid combination of caffeination, hydration, and intoxication really is the perfect triumvirate.

Naively, I thought this idiosyncratic drink habit of mine was invisible. But friends and family members delight in calling attention to my beverage addiction. I'm not sure whether it's my lengthy drink order that attracts attention or the fact that my thirst-quenching threesome encroaches on my dinner companions' table space, but my tablemates can't resist making comments like, "There she goes again with her *three* drinks!" Sometimes my friends even jump in to order for me. Nevertheless, I'm undaunted. I believe in my sipping strategy.

I was surprised, however, when my daughter-in-law mentioned that I had liberated her beverage habits. "I thought you could only order one drink at a time. It didn't occur to me to order multiples. I feel so free." And I almost fell off the kitchen stool on Christmas Eve one year when I overheard my then forty-eight-year-old stepson quoting me to his friends: "Caffeination, hydration, intoxication. It's the perfect dinner drink combination." My friend Susan told me that her family calls this kind of drink ordering, "Doing a Liz." You can imagine my delight.

Ordering multiple beverages hardly constitutes rule breaking, but it does step outside the dining norm. And you just never know when your little break with convention might inspire others.

BBLB Manual of Maxims #4:
"Don't be afraid to break with convention. It is liberating and might just inspire others."

BEIGE-I-FYING MY HOUSE

When my husband and I decided to put our house of thirty-two years on the market, our realtor suggested we hire a "house editor" for guidance in neutralizing and decluttering our home. I whined about repainting my colorful walls beige, removing my funky light fixture, and cutting our art collection in half. But the staging objective, according to my realtor, was to make my house as marketable as possible for potential buyers (translated: my frenetic ADD design aesthetic might cost us the sale.).

I actually liked this decorator/house editor, and in spite of my whining, I invited her back a year later for advice on redecorating the townhouse we purchased after selling our home. Downsizing had resulted in our having to cram a dining room table, an old sofa, an oversized chair, and various other Choctaw Trail relics into a smaller space. I was in dire need of professional advice.

I'm a big fan of consultants. I am a consultant and appreciate it when clients actually listen to the advice I offer. So, I listened to Sherrie even though she banned me from buying even one piece of furniture, rug, or lamp containing a speck of color. Everything had to be gray, cream, or beige, and I found myself agreeing to pay too much money for a cream-colored sofa and a neutral area rug. The sales rep at the furniture store told me that in his fifteen-year relationship with our decorator he had never seen her allow a client to purchase a patterned armchair (But we insisted.). Her mantra was, "The neutral choices you make will enhance your artwork," and she insisted, "The eye needs a place to rest." Grudgingly, I listened to her.

Later, when I needed help redecorating the very small kitchen in our townhouse, I invited Sherrie back for what turned out to be the final time. As before, I listened to her recommendations even though she thwarted me at every turn. "White" was her relentless refrain. White quartz counter tops, white cabinets, and a white backsplash. I tentatively broached the notion of "interesting" tile for the backsplash.

"What do you mean, *interesting*?" she asked, breathing out what felt like disdain.

Stumbling and stammering I said something weak like, "I'm not sure, but I'll know it when I see it."

I even behaved like a petulant child during a shopping outing when I sensed that she was mocking my ignorance. Eventually, I submitted to her mandates and ended up with a completely white kitchen. Let me make it known that I do believe Sherrie has class and taste. "Your kitchen will be timeless and great for resale," she reassured me.

As soon as she was out the door, I began coloring up the kitchen. Within five hours I'd added a red toaster, purple clock, and a folk-art painting featuring colorful coffee cups.

This experience reminded me that Be Brave. Lose the Beige! is about *being brave*. In the case of my redecorating efforts, I was trying to be brave about change. Even at my age, I want to be open to changes and transformations. Doesn't mean I'll stick to them though.

BBLB Manual of Maxims #5:
"Be brave and open to changes and life transitions."

BBLB RECAP

Be Brave, Lose the Beige! is a philosophy, a way of perceiving your world. Fundamental to this philosophy is creativity and creative thinking. Football coach Vince Lombardi urged his players to "run for the daylight; find the open spaces." This is a good metaphor for creativity. Thinking creatively means finding the cracks of light in the darkness. Slip through them into the unknown or untried.

Creativity can be risky. It's scary to sing in public, to show someone our writing, to present a new idea for a business; unveiling our creations exposes us in much the same way as dropping our drawers. But challenging airport protocols and ordering multiple beverages helps put us in the driver's seat. So creative thinking is an excellent partner in the quest to retain control while navigating this aging journey. It's fun and freeing to color outside lines that have constrained us for much of our lives, and creativity offers us a lightheartedness our aching backs and clogged arteries keep trying to steal.

EXERCISE YOUR CREATIVITY #1:

DOODLE FOR YOUR NOODLE

An easy and unintimidating way to exercise your creative muscles is doodling. Doodling is playful and the epitome of creative freedom. Boring meetings and phone conversations offer prime doodling opportunities, and don't think that entertaining yourself this way constitutes rude behavior. Sunni Brown, a longtime doodler and author of *The Doodle Revolution*, is convinced doodling isn't mindless but actually *engages* the mind. She contends that doodling can help in problem solving and aid in memory retention.[8]

When you find yourself in a boring lecture or Zoom call, doodling may actually help you focus and pay attention. John F. Kennedy doodled sailboats, Ronald Reagan cowboys. Hey, whatever helps a president stay focused and pay attention—I say, "Do it!"

Doodling is fun, relaxing, and requires no artistic training or special tools. Something to doodle with and something to doodle on are all you need.

Spend the next ten minutes giving it a try. Grab a pen or pencil. Pens come in various tip thicknesses; colored pencils make for colorful doodles. If staring at a blank page stunts your creativity, try dividing your page into four or more sections. Your lines can be wavy or straight and ultimately become a part of the design. Start with some basic shapes—ovals, loops, triangles, even leaves and flowers. Draw any geometric shapes you feel drawn to. No one else needs to see the results of this creative effort. The simple repetitive nature of drawing patterns is relaxing, relieves stress, and can boost creative confidence.

Happy doodling.

CHAPTER 2:

The 'Tweener Generation

"Baby Boomers are the slice of boloney sandwiched between caring for aging parents and parenting adult children."
—KITCHENS

The term 'tweener has been hijacked to reference kids between the ages of nine and twelve. I say that "Tweener Generation" more aptly applies to Lady Boomers. We're the slice of boloney sandwiched between two demanding generations. The demands of these two generations—our mothers and our children—managed to mute many of our Magenta impulses.

DEMANDING GENERATION #1: Our mothers. Yes, of course our moms are or were great. The climate in which they became moms, however, didn't encourage self-actualization or the fulfillment of personal ambitions. 1960s television portrayed married women as happy homemakers, and if these women *did* work outside the home, it was typically as a secretary, teacher, or nurse. Marriage bars, a practice adopted in the late nineteenth century and continuing into the 1960s, restricted married women from employment in many professions. So how did many of them handle that restriction? By thrusting their thwarted ambitions onto the shoulders of their daughters. At a young age, I remember feeling the weight of my mother's disappointments. She repeatedly recounted her dream of singing opera on stage, but her young marriage and three children curtailed that dream. I know my two brothers didn't share the weight of this emotional responsibility, as evidenced by their shock when my parents announced their impending divorce. *Haven't you lived in the same house with me*, I wondered at the time. *Did you not see her tears and hear her sighs?*

My mother wasn't shy about sharing what she'd missed by failing to marry her high school boyfriend. Apparently, Arthur was smart, ambitious, faithful, and Jewish. I guess I honored her wishes by marrying someone smart, ambitious, faithful, and Jewish.

Many baby boomer girls and women I've met over the years feel much the same way about being saddled with their mother's disappointments. "My mom and my mom's friends weren't shy about sharing their regrets and disappointments in front of us," my friend Susan told me. Susan, like many Lady Boomers, was sent an implicit memo, "Do what I didn't have the chance to do." While I sound like I'm indicting these women we love so much, I'm also excusing them because the societal expectations in place at the time deserve a lot of blame.

The mothers of boomer girls were the women featured in the television show, *Mad Men*. Set in the 1960s, the show focused on the men who ran advertising and public relations firms on New York's Madison Avenue. We were given a glimpse of the frustration endured by their wives and other women on the show. Betty Draper, the wife of the show's protagonist, is a Bryn Mawr graduate who stays home with her three children and spends much of her time smoking cigarettes and daydreaming. The show depicted her as someone who spent more time on her chaise lounge dreaming about what might have been than assuming responsibility for the emotional lives of her children. In one episode of *Mad Men*, Betty Draper's father dies, and all the focus is on Betty and her devastation. No attention is paid to the emotional reactions experienced by her eleven-year-old daughter, Sally, who, in the final scene, is shown grieving alone in the dark under the dining room table. Friends and I related to that emotional scenario.

DEMANDING GENERATION 2: Our kids. The other slice of bread forming this sandwich is our enabling behaviors toward our children, often well into their adulthood. We are the generation that engaged in self-esteem parenting, focusing on building our children's confidence.

When I was a young mother, I was committed to being a good parent to my daughter and son, but I also wanted and needed to earn a living. Some of us mothers were lucky, as flexible schedules allowed us to attend school plays and afternoon tennis matches. Many midnights, however, found us hunched over computers playing career catch-up following evenings filled with homework, dinner preparation, and family time. But we felt driven to try and "have it all" and were guided by messages like those of Betty Friedan, who preached a message of empowerment in *The Feminine Mystique*: "We can no longer ignore that voice in women's heads that says, 'I want more than my husband, and my kids, and my home.'"[1] I suspect the diverted dreams of our mothers influenced that desire to have it all. We said

23

to ourselves, *I want more than a husband, children, and a home, and I'm going to get it.*

But boy, working *and* raising children is hard. And finding trustworthy, affordable childcare can be the working mother's nightmare. I still suffer from episodic PTSD flashbacks remembering the difficulty finding and keeping good child-minders for my children. "Electrocuted" would be an apt description of how I felt each time one of them quit. A few were actually reliable and didn't quit without notice. A few had decent cars that didn't pollute the carpool line at school. (My kids were banned from drop-off in the drive-through line because Jewish Community Center staff were being asphyxiated by the belching exhaust fumes gushing from our nanny's 1975 Chevrolet Impala.) One or two *weren't* engaged in high drama with unfaithful boyfriends or estranged husbands. The security of knowing your children are safe and well cared for and the ability to get to your office on time each morning is—well, let's just say it—priceless!

The upshot of our 'tweener status? Guilt. Guilt for leaving our kids in the arms of caregivers as we rushed off to work each day and for giving our Gen Xer's latchkey childhoods. The two sides of this generational sandwich— actualizing our moms' deferred dreams and fulfilling our own motherly roles—laid the groundwork for postponing ourselves and depleted much of our sass and color.

OUR MOMS: OUR MODELS OF MOTHERHOOD

According to a 2015 Pew Research Center study, half of mothers in the 1960s stayed home full time. And while some of those stay-at-home moms might have wanted more for themselves, they didn't face the competing roles conundrum many of their daughters experienced when they became parents, a conundrum that called for us to both pursue a career *and* behave like the *Leave It to Beaver* role models ingrained in our brains.

Christmas ran through my mother's veins like Santa's reindeer racing through the night trying to meet their early morning deadline. What the family budget lacked, her drive and enthusiasm made up for. Christmas in the Lang house felt as magical as Santa's workshop, complete with the Scotch Pine tree we cut down and festooned with colorful lights and handmade ornaments. We baked cookies and melted paraffin for candles to give as gifts. She made the holidays special. Mom's impoverished early years had denied her much of the Yuletide fun and festivities her friends might have taken for granted. She made up for this early lack with her own family.

My mother spent early years in Omega, Georgia, a place where opportunities go to die. And even worse, she was the daughter of the town drunk. Buster Woodall spent many Saturday nights in jail following evenings of drinking and carousing. Then, dusting himself off early in the morning, he would put on his cleanest dirty shirt and ask for forgiveness at his local Southern Baptist church.

At thirteen, my mother escaped her small-town fate by moving to Orlando with her paternal grandmother. Mom's years attending what was then the only high school in town introduced her to a bigger world and ultimately to my father, a sailor from Long Island, New York. In Orlando, she kept company with the children of the city's nobility—the publisher of the city's two daily newspapers, a real estate scion, bankers, and successful Jewish merchants. She spoke of her high school popularity and conveyed her expectation that I achieve a comparable social status within my own sphere as well.

She loved opera and the classics. She would don her imitation pearls, white gloves, and best dress and take us to what passed as a concert hall to hear symphonies performed. She aspired to a bigger life, but her premature death at forty-nine cut short many of those aspirations. I didn't have the chance to have adult conversations with my mom about her early history and mothering models. I think understanding her history might have helped me understand its impact upon me. Instead, I was left with the 1960s motherhood model stamped on my forehead.

The children of many boomers were enrolled in afterschool programs or greeted in the afternoons by babysitters or nannies. This was a contrast from the way we were greeted by our *Leave it to Beaver* moms. The upshot? More guilt for us. So, since we couldn't always "be there" physically, Boomer moms chose to be present in other ways—emotionally, psychologically, and even monetarily. And that behavior lasted well into our children's adulthood.

THE ONE-HOUR EMPTY NEST

We managed to survive childcare challenges, homework, curfew controversies, and totaled Toyotas (and my current husband being sued for a million dollars as a result of said totaled Toyota driven by my long-haired son who was deemed to be at fault). As they crested toward sixteen on the Yellow Brick Road of youth, the Emerald City (in the form of college or other employment training) beckoned teenagers anxious to try on freedom for the first time.

"I'm never coming back to Orlando," was a refrain we heard from two of the three teens occupying our home. (Our Brady Bunch consisted of my two children and my husband's son.) "I can't wait to leave home! This is going to be great!" Hearing these kinds of proclamations, parents experience myriad emotions—we become teary at the prospect of our babies leaving the nest, and at the same time we find ourselves villain-fatigued from thwarting adolescent ambitions.

"What will we do with ourselves once they're gone?" Lady Boomers wailed. As it turned out, many of us didn't have to struggle with that question for long.

A phenomenon called "boomerang kids" impacted a quarter of us. Because all three of my children boomeranged home at one point or another, I felt entitled to come up with an operational definition for this syndrome:

Boo-mer-ang kids (noun): those young adults who leave home with youthful idealism and excitement about the adventures awaiting them, only to ricochet back to their rooms when life out of the nest, with its pesky responsibilities, thwarts their efforts at independence.

When my husband and I deposited my youngest son on the doorstep of George Washington University in Washington DC in mid-August 2001, we became empty-nested for the first time in our eleven-year marriage; we like to say we were empty nesters for less than an hour.

My husband and I were driving back to our Florida home when my daughter—at the time in her third year of college in North Carolina—called to say, "I'm coming home, Mom. I've decided to drop out of school. You won't have to worry about having an empty nest!"

All I could say was, "Let me call you back, Honey." We pulled over at a rest stop, and I bought a pack of cigarettes.

As it turned out, my daughter was suffering from a love affair gone bad. "Bad" is actually an understatement. The abusive boyfriend had been in the country illegally from Tunisia. The FBI suspected him of having terrorist cell connections and subsequently deported him. When the horrors of 9/11 happened just a month later, it all hit a little too close to home. Then, in the midst of that emotional upheaval, my son, newly ensconced in his freshman dorm in DC, was kicked out for smoking weed. He spent a couple of nomadic months roaming from bed to borrowed bed until he was eventually sent home for three semesters. And just like that, I went from having an empty nest to "no room at the inn."

It was during that fateful fall that I realized (as I was spending time in bed with the covers pulled over my head—watching a lot of episodes of *Sex and the City* and *Antiques Roadshow*) I needed a survival strategy. Anxiety had stripped me of my color. I was in a beige state of mind.

A long dormant desire to teach at-risk teens to make pots instead of smoke pot propelled me off my pillows. (Maybe I should have thanked my children for the extra inspiration?) With ten years of pottery experience under my belt, I wanted to use clay to help kids in underserved communities develop creative thinking skills through the arts.

Together with three other Lady Boomer friends, I

launched a program called "The Jeremiah Project." The name was inspired by a verse from the Old Testament book of Jeremiah, ". . . then the Lord said, 'Just like the clay in the potter's hand, so are you in my hand.'" Our after school and summer pottery program reached out to at-risk middle school age students. I guess my strategy for coping with a national crisis and BKS (Boomerang Kid Syndrome) was to focus on something bigger than my immediate world. And that strategy was successful; the conception, planning, and fundraising for this project gave me back my power. During that tumultuous time, I felt control over some portion of my life. This was just one of the times in my life when creative thinking converted a crisis into a positive and constructive outcome.

THE PURLOINED PIGSKIN

Who likes football? According to a January 2020 post in the sports blog, Sports Virsa, football is the most popular American sport.[2] I confess to not being one of these ardent fans. However, one of my prized possessions is a game ball from the Outback Bowl played at Raymond James Stadium in Tampa, Florida, on January 1, 2010. The game matched the Northwestern University Wildcats against the Auburn University Tigers.

I rarely follow football. I don't know names of quarter-backs or coaches or the difference between a safety and a wide receiver (although I'm feeling pretty good about myself for even recognizing these positions. Ok, truth squad time—I actually Googled "football positions." But I digress). Nor do I understand the rules of foot-ball. For example, why are four downs needed to make a first down? The redundancy baffles me. I do, however, nominally follow one college football team, namely the Northwestern University Wildcats, my son's graduate school alma mater. He absolutely loves this Big Ten team, and because I love him, I love what he loves.

My son, his then girlfriend (now wife), his dad (my former husband), another Northwestern alum, and I gamely arose at 7:00 a.m. New Year's Day to make the hour and a half drive through pelting rain to attend the 11:00 Outback Bowl game in Tampa, Florida. We joined a sea of purple paraphernalia when we took our seats in the end zone.

It rained. And rained. And rained. Northwestern did not fare well. The players from Auburn University dwarfed the NU team. We were down by two touchdowns at halftime. Things were looking bleak for our beloved team. During halftime, as we dried out under cover at the concession stand, I suggested leaving after the third quarter if the weather conditions and playing didn't improve. Even my son, a die-hard, loyal fan, agreed.

But during the second half, the game and weather did improve. Ponchos and parkas were discarded. NU came back in the third quarter and tied the score. The fans in Northwestern purple launched themselves into a frenzy, jumping up and down and high-fiving total strangers. Auburn scored again, however, and the kicker lined up to kick the extra point. The field crew, distracted by Auburn's excessive celebration, failed to raise the net behind the goal post in time to catch the ball, so the pigskin sailed over the end zone, over the goal post, and into my son's seat. Fans all around scrambled for the ball. Amid the chaos, David scooped it up and tucked it beneath our pile of ponchos.

It's a weird feeling having an entire stadium look in

your direction anticipating the return of the game ball. But our band of brothers decided to do nothing, which seemed to work because the game resumed with a new ball. After about ten minutes, I said to my son, "Why don't I put the ball in my backpack? No one will think a fifty-seven-year-old woman is interested in keeping a football." So I did, transferring my wallet, used Kleenexes, iPhone, tube of oozing moisture lotion, keys, etc., elsewhere to accommodate the bulky ball. I then proceeded to watch an exciting quarter of football, albeit with a pounding heart.

I swear, my son was not raised to steal. Neither was I. Neither was our fellow co-conspirator, his dad, at the time a circuit judge. We simply assumed the same rules for baseball games applied to football games. At a baseball game, you get to keep the errant ball if it comes your way. And who cares anyway? College football is a multi-billion-dollar industry in which everyone but the players make tons of money. I assumed they could afford extra balls.

Well, count me wrong in that assumption. In short order we heard a booming voice behind us say, "Somebody's going to jail tonight if that football isn't returned." We turned around to see a police officer threading his way through the end zone, pointing an accusing finger at my son. The policeman looked like a southern cop straight out of Hollywood's central casting—burly and big bellied, scowling, and speaking with a southern drawl. David's outstretched hands were empty as was the rain gear he held up for inspection. After questioning adjacent fans, he turned a suspicious eye on me. I'm told I looked like a flasher as I opened and closed my raincoat as if to say, "I have nothing to hide." The officer pointed to my backpack saying, "I assume there're just clothes in that bag of yours." I don't think I responded. I can't remember. I was so scared. I actually would have been happy to return the stupid ball at that point. This fun little lark was fast losing its appeal. But at that point I would have looked like an idiot pulling the football out of my backpack. Meanwhile, the cop persisted in his menacing intimidation. "I'd like to take one of these entitled brats down to the station," he groused. Interestingly, none of the surrounding fans gave us up. I guess screaming your head off with a group of strangers, all wearing the same colors, really creates a bond.

I was a wreck. My stomach was churning. I pulled my lawyer/current judge/former husband over to my side and said, "Here's a dollar. I've officially hired you to represent me." Meanwhile, my current husband's last words as I left the house rang in my ears: "Have fun but be careful." I decided to exercise discretion and return the ball to one of the four over-zealous police officers now standing at the railing above us.

But just before I gave up the goods, something odd happened. *Nothing* happened. A raucous celebration had broken out when Northwestern scored another touchdown forcing the game into overtime. Adjacent fans were screaming and jumping up and down, distracting the cops from our caper. Maybe I wouldn't have to make the walk of shame after all, and maybe we could actually keep this hard-earned ball. The game finally ended. I stripped off my Northwestern purple so I'd no longer look like a fan, and my lawyer/ judge/former husband and I, with the purloined pigskin in tow, exited the stands one way as my son and co-alums departed in the opposite direction. We were immediately swept up into the crowd and out of the stadium. As we made our way to the car, I refused to say a word about the crime for fear of being overheard. And I didn't hear my cell phone ringing as my son frantically tried to reach me, thinking we'd been stopped or seized. Now that I think about it, our level of paranoia might have been out of proportion relative to the potential consequences. I was probably experiencing flashbacks, harkening back to a 1960s fear of "the fuzz."

Eventually, we all rendezvoused back at our car, but no one was allowed to open the offending backpack until we were out of Hillsborough County. I had visions of roadblocks set up to search departing cars for the filched football.

The next day, still shaken from our petty larceny, the fabulous five signed the ball to commemorate the experience. I signed as "Lightfingers Liz Kitchens." I guess my propensity for selective rule-breaking was in force that day. (Obviously my son inherited this tendency as well.) While admittedly nerve wracking, the events of that day are woven into the rich tapestry of my life. An ordinary event became a memorable family experience. Maybe all that purple in the stands inspired my Magenta self to peek out.

Oh, by the way . . . the Auburn Tigers ultimately won in overtime 38 to 35. Damn.

CALL US ENABLERS-IN-CHIEF

As I mentioned, the boomer parenting style is a departure from that of our parents. My parents—and from what I have observed, my friends' parents—were much less involved in our lives than we boomers have been in our own children's. But Lady Boomers signed a silent maternal contract, the clauses of which mandated we would be deeply involved in our kids' lives well beyond the age of maturity. We fostered an environment in which our grown children frequently turn to us for guidance and advice. And we like helping them solve or brainstorm their way through problems. We value maintaining the connection; we might even be addicted to the feeling of being needed.

But don't kid yourselves, this kind of prolonged parenting can be emotionally exhausting. I remember confessing to a friend that I felt like a piece of saltwater taffy I'd been stretched so much by my adult darlings. I was recounting my then thirty-five-year-old daughter's SOS calls asking for help navigating a prickly work situation. Her egomaniacal boss had taken credit for the five-hundred-thousand-dollar grant Tracy had just secured for the agency.

Is our mothering behavior noble and selfless or enabling? Are our codependent relationships with kids an excuse for avoiding concentrating on our own next steps?

LET'S ABOLISH MOTHER'S DAY

Do you know what I think would be liberating for Lady Boomers? (Hmm, I might have given the answer away with that subtitle.) Abolishing Mother's Day! I can't speak for Gen X, Millennial, or Gen Z Moms, but I believe I can channel Lady Boomers' attitudes toward this issue. Mother's Day is ostensibly the day we pay homage to our mothers. If you're a mother, you might assume the day is about you and your needs. The greeting card industry, social media, and television ads certainly promote this notion. Perhaps this is an accurate representation for some. But also true is the fact that we are daughters and in some cases grandmothers. So already the day is fraught with complications.

As women, we are prone to feeling responsible for holidays and special occasions, even those supposedly devoted to us. More often than not, the day finds us hosting family dinners, running errands for others, or schlepping to spend the day with relatives. (A few years ago, a friend confided she spent the morning of Mother's Day perusing Craig's List and emailing possible subletting opportunities for her daughter who was moving to Denver for three months.)

Let me pause for a moment and pose another question: How pampered and relaxed do you feel as Mother's Day comes to a close? Like many moms, I have spent some perfectly wonderful Mother's Days, but generally, they've not been focused on my needs. One year, I had the good fortune to share the day with my darling daughter, who treated me to brunch at the Baltimore Museum of Art, but then we spent the remainder of the day searching for a new apartment *for her*. If it's Mother's Day what are we doing doting on everyone else?

Part B of this Mother's Day overview has to do with pesky expectations. Just as Charlie Brown vows not to get tricked once again by Lucy moving the football, we get tricked into thinking each year will be different. We head into each Mother's Day with high hopes that: (1) the kids will remember the day—the second Sunday of May (although aren't we entitled to a designated date so we don't leave this to chance?!); (2) at least one of them will plan a gathering, including food, where we can relax and spend time together; (3) the Happy Mother's Day call will be the first one they make that day; (4) maybe the ding-dong of the doorbell will usher in a bouquet of blossoms from our babies; (5) they will understand the way the postal service works and our card or package will arrive in a timely fashion.

And expectations go both ways. There is a great deal of pressure on moms to react with sufficient enthusiastic appreciation for our kids' demonstrations of appreciation on Mother's Day. Opening gifts should be accompanied by appropriate levels of squealing, wide-mouthed smiles, kissing, and hugging. One year, my father bought my mother ice trays and an electric can opener for Mother's Day gifts. My mother failed the appreciation test by locking herself in her room for the remainder of the day. My brothers and I were devastated by my mother's reaction. Of course, we blamed her rather than my clueless father for our hurt feelings. Boomer moms simply aren't allowed to react in such a dramatic and unappreciative manner. We would be besieged with guilt should we respond honestly.

As a boomer mom, I feel as you do, no doubt, that *I have the greatest kids in the world.* (It's actually mandated in the motherhood manual that we make this statement.) They have performed many loving gestures throughout the last forty-plus years, my favorite of which occurred in 2014.

My son and daughter-in-law FaceTimed Mother's Day evening. Expecting them to chide me about my whiny "I've Got the Mother's Day Blues" blog I had posted earlier in the day, I was surprised to find two giggly thirty-one-year-olds looking like they had just swallowed a couple of canaries. "We took a test, and it looks like we are pregnant," my daughter-in-law announced. I'm not sure I realized I was screaming for what must have been a minute. Now it was my turn to be fidgety and giggly.

Months of ultrasounds and doctor's visits reassured them about the viability of their impending baby girl,

Maya Rose. Looking back, I realized my children gave me a perennial rose for Mother's Day.

Aside from soon-to-be grandchildren, the greatest Mother's Day present is sharing the day with our kids, but that's hard to do when they live far away—in my case, one in northern Illinois and the other in southern Illinois. The other injuries—like the card arriving on the following Monday or the call in the late afternoon, almost as an afterthought (and I'm guessing it most definitely is)—is small stuff compared to their absences. Absences are another reason to abolish the holiday. The missing is even more pronounced on this day of honoring moms. It's hurtful to observe other families gathering to celebrate in parks or restaurants. Those of us with kids living far away and those who have wanted but have been unable to have children probably feel left out.

I was FaceTiming with my four-year-old grandson one May day in 2021. "It's only two more days until Mother's Day!" he gleefully exclaimed.

"What are you getting Mommy?" I naively asked.

"I don't know," he said, "but *I'm* getting a Lego Harry Potter set." I couldn't help it. I began to shake my head and laugh. "What's so funny, Jozy," Ru asked failing to see any humor in our exchange. I started singing, "And the beat goes on . . . and the beat goes on . . ."

THE CHRISTMAS KEY LIME PIE CAPER

One thing my family loves, especially at holiday gatherings, is playing games: board games, scavenger hunts, charades, etc. We love a good challenge. So when my son presented me with a challenge for the Christmas holidays a couple of years ago, I took it on like a military mission.

"Mom, I've been thinking." (Uh oh, that often means I'll need my credit card.) "Since you're coming up to Chicago for Christmas, you should bring up something particularly representative of Florida." *Am I not representative enough? I was actually born in the state. Won't I do?* I wondered silently.

"Okay, I'll bite. What are you thinking?"

"I'm thinking you should bring up a key lime pie for Christmas dinner. We're having Katie's family over, and a Florida dessert would be an excellent addition."

"Do you expect me to make the pie?" I asked, slightly incredulous at his failure to recall my lack of baking skills.

"Uh, no, of course not. But you know all the locations in Orlando where they sell the real-deal key lime pies," he said in recognition of my true skill: discernment. *Why bake something when there are perfectly wonderful people to bake it for you for about the same price as it would cost to buy all the ingredients?* Not to mention the value to my psyche! Baking requires precision, a skill not in abundance in my being.)

"Uh, how do you propose I get it there?" I asked in a tentative voice.

"You'll be on Southwest so you can just carry it on. In fact, maybe you should bring two in case one doesn't make it." My husband by this point was busily Googling how to have key lime pies shipped from Florida to Chicago. Since it was already two days before Christmas, the availability of pies for a timely air-delivery seemed unlikely.

"This is impossible," Jim weighed in. I must interject here that I often overrule my dear husband's votes in favor of my kids'. I'm not proud of this fact, but I don't think I'm alone in this tendency. My Lady Boomer friends also seem to routinely subordinate their spouses' needs and wills to those of their adult children.

"I think we're up to this challenge," I argued. A holiday poem inspired our mission:

'Twas two days before Christmas when my cell phone began ringing,
When I saw my son's name, my heart started singing.

Visions of key lime pies were dancing in David's head,
So, it was his mamma's job to get that boy fed.

Mrs. Santa and her elf began their search,
In hopes of finding some tropical desserts.

"Eureka!" I shouted and called out the name,
"Charlie's Bakery's the place, and the pies have acclaim."

They're going fast so no time to waste,
"Please save them," I begged, and we left in great haste.

Slipping and sliding on the slick Florida streets,
We risked life and limb for our citrusy sweets.

Two key lime pies stored safely in the sled,
The second task became finding them beds.

The Bed, Bath & Beyond promised they had carriers,
So away we sailed, only to find one more barrier.

"We only have one," the nice manager said.

But a wink of his eye and a twist of his head soon made me know I had nothing to dread.

"Our location in Casselberry (thirty minutes away) has plenty.
So, please don't worry about coming up empty."

So up to the house top (or Bed Bath and Beyond) the coursers we flew,
In pursuit of the carriers, though we just needed two.

We laughed when we saw them, in spite of ourselves,
So much was accomplished by these right jolly old elves.

Coolers and ice kept pies cold for transport,
As we flew toward Chicago's Midway airport.

One hundred dollars and three hours of holiday traffic
May seem to you just a little bit drastic.

But the pies were a hit and pleased was the crowd,
It made me happy my son was so proud.

Yes, there was the short notice; yes, we spent additional dollars on the heels of Christmas purchases; yes, we spent three hours driving in a downpour amid holiday traffic; and, of course, my husband's vote was vetoed in favor of my son's request. Our kids continue to make demands well into their adulthood. More often than not, moms comply. We can, however, reframe the experience rather than being victimized by it. In our case, we transformed the excursion into a scavenger hunt, which turned out to be a fun, memorable, mini adventure. The caper even provided fodder for a story I posted on my BBLB blog. Lady Boomer friends chuckled in recognition, seeing themselves in the tale.

BBLB Manual of Maxims #6:
"Don't be a victim."

Convert kid demands and other annoyances into experiences that benefit you too. I love a good game. A holiday scavenger hunt was just up my alley.

THE MAGGIANO'S MANEUVER

You may imagine the efforts expended in my key lime pie caper were only to please my son. But I really do love celebrating the holidays, especially Christmas. When I contemplated converting to Judaism in my former life, I was perfectly willing to celebrate Rosh Hashanah and spend the day fasting in quiet contemplation on Yom Kippur. However, giving up Christmas was never an option. I'm obsessed with Christmas decorations, Christmas movies, and Christmas music. Given the name of this book, it goes without saying, I'm wild about color. All colors. The bolder the better. And Christmas brings the color.

I also love seeing the way my son continues to tease his sister in a manner his own daughter and wife will not permit. The primordial family familiarity bred into their DNA allows for this familiar interaction. I enjoy seeing my daughter interacting with her niece and nephew and witnessing the kind of father my son has become.

But as much as I cherish the season, this is the time of year I'm most likely to lose my Magenta. The irony of losing one's color during a season brimming with blues, reds, and greens is not lost on me.

A 2016 *New York Times* article coined a term for the stress of expectations surrounding holidays: "Family Jet Lag."

The holidays mean large extended family gatherings, hours of cooking and a group of people who don't typically interact in person, all confined to one location and trying to act festive. It's the reality show version of your family. When you return from your holiday visit, you may be exhausted for days afterward, finding it hard to focus and return to your regular routine. It feels as if you took the red-eye from Phoenix, but in reality, it was a quick one-hour flight from Cleveland.[3]

Expectations permeate the holidays. Expectations for marriage, children, and career advancements thread their way into cooking conversations and gift-giving. Those pesky expectations are as prevalent as the pumpkin (or key lime) pie. And they go both ways. It's not just parents projecting expectations on to their offspring; our kids have their own expectations of us, too.

My education on the topic of expectations was expanded during a holiday trip to Chicago just before Covid shut down the world.

Our kids surprised us with a variety of treats during that trip. I received a colorful pop art piece of luggage designed by Brazilian artist Romero Britto. And the kids attempted to winterize my forever-cold husband with a college-themed sweatshirt and hat to make the harsh Chicago weather more bearable. Jim's stocking included a gift card to Maggiano's, a favorite family restaurant in Skokie, Illinois.

IT IS A BIT STARTLING when we realize our children are actually launched. I don't know what your definition of launched might look like, but mine includes the following criteria: They are able to pay their own car insurance and cell phone bills; they can afford their own airline travel; they don't require your co-signature on a home improvement loan; and the presents they give you are an upgrade from the afterthoughts of yesteryear. We were thrilled with our Christmas bounty.

Jim and I planned to put his stocking stuffer to use following a weekend of child-minding during that holiday stay. Shrugging into coats and scarves, we heard, "Um, would you mind bringing food back for us too?"

"Of course, text us your order," I replied to my son.

"He just can't resist enjoying part of your Christmas present," I chuckled to my husband as we got in the car.

Jim laughed too. "Remember how last year he gave me a Binny's Liquor Store gift card, which I was strongly encouraged to use to buy booze for his in-laws' Christmas Eve celebration?"

Well, we enjoyed a delightful lunch at Maggiano's and dutifully ordered takeout for the family. When we presented our gift card to the server she informed us, "This can't be used until next year." The waitress did not seem amused by our guffawing. Our Christmas present ended up costing us $90. Our kids, meanwhile, would enjoy our gift card in the new year since it would have expired prior to our return visit.

Remember BBLB Manual of Maxims #7:
"Cultivate a sense of humor."

It will come in handy.

Even though they may be launched, kids still love languishing in the luxury of their parent's attention and indulgences. No one loves them quite like their moms, but mothers do have the capacity to hold concurrent views of their adult children. While recognizing the self-centeredness of their demands, we simultaneously recognize their goodness and serve as containers for those co-existing perceptions. But all those emotions take up space and threaten to crowd our own needs and wants, so it's important to protect those parts of ourselves that give our lives meaning and contribute to our wellbeing. I'm still far from proficient at setting boundaries. But when I do, I notice fuchsia and turquoise tiptoeing back in to color up my spirit.

I have to admit my color had faded to the beige end of the spectrum by the conclusion of that holiday trip. As we headed out the door to the airport and home, I heard, "Oh, by the way, are you still down with paying for half of our airline flights when we come to Florida in January?" *Did I mention I wasn't proficient at setting my own boundaries monetary or otherwise?* Do what I say, not what I do.

PARENTING IS NOT A POPULARITY CONTEST, OR IS IT?

BBLB Manual of Maxims #8:
"Parenting is not a popularity contest."

I need to tattoo this maxim on my forehead! My former husband and I have a running joke as to which one of us our children like best. We jostle with each other at airport pickups for the first hug from an arriving child. Our kids tease each other in their own version of the Hauser/ Kitchens Family Love Competition.

"Ha! I won," my daughter will exclaim on my birthday morning. "I called you first. I love you more than David does."

Maybe other families aren't so competitive? While I choose to believe this is good natured gamesmanship, I know I'm responsible for this dynamic. I actually want to be popular with my kids. They are my favorite people. I want to please them. But news flash! *Their* children have a way of vindicating grandparents.

A MOTHER'S CHILD

My son and I were cooking breakfast one Sunday morning during a Chicago visit. Quite familiar with his daughter's love of the film *Frozen*, David cracked a corny joke about the Olaf pancakes he was preparing. Maya rolled her six-year-old eyes, communicating how unfunny she found her father to be. "Dad, you're so lame," he murmured to me, mimicking Maya. Since I find my son's witticisms to be hilarious, I was surprised by his self-deprecation.

Before bed that night I wrote about this exchange in my journal, concocting the following hypothetical scenario about generational perspectives:

> *David excitedly announces to his family:* "I just got invited to throw the first pitch out for a White Sox game because of my therapy work with some of their players."

Daughter's reaction: "Huh?" She responds, barely glancing up to make eye contact. When she finally does, the glazed-over look in her eyes reveals her lack of interest in this honor. She has bigger fish to fry. Tomorrow is carnival day at camp and she's weighing her clothing and show-and-tell options.

Wife's reaction: "That's nice. What's the date?" she asks, reaching for her color-coded calendar, dreading trying to fit in yet another appointment. Her day planner resembles a work of art, resplendent with colorful neon Post-it Notes consuming entire day blocks. "Oh shoot, I've got clients that day and a Parent-Teacher conference that night. You know, you should really be there, too. Our family and our income are more important than a ceremonial gig for work you've already done and been paid for." Muttering under her breath, "He can be so self-involved sometimes."

My reaction: "What?!!! Seriously?!!! That is totally cool. Can I come?" I beg, already clicking on the Southwest app to book a flight. "Ann and John have the baseball package on Spectrum. I'll make sure they watch the Sox-Orioles game that day. Susan loves baseball. Maybe I'll have her come with me. I want to get plenty of pics to post on Facebook and Instagram. I'm so proud of you, David."

The reactions described are from the vantage point of someone who has lived through each of these life stages.

And recording this fictional scenario helped me to realize the striking differences in generational perspectives.

WHEN MY SON WAS BORN, a friend told me that moms tend to think their sons' shit doesn't stink. This line became family lore when David was younger. "Now don't go thinking your poop doesn't stink, because it does," I would counsel.

"No, Mom, I promise it doesn't," he would protest. "And besides, my body odor smells like roses."

There actually may be some truth to the adage, as more than a few moms I know are raptly attentive to stories and accomplishments shared by their children (sons *and* daughters). It makes me think we will always play the role of lead cheerleaders in our children's lives (no wonder in-laws resent us!).

BBLB Manual of Maxims #9:
"Yes, your children's shit really does stink."

A TOAST TO MOTHERHOOD

A few years ago, on December 31, as is our custom, my husband and I conducted a year-in-review sitting in our Adirondack chairs sipping wine in shorts and flip-flops in Florida's eighty-five-degree weather.

Jim said he wanted to kiss the year a thankful goodbye, saying how grateful he was for certain academic and professional successes. His book, *The Four Pillars of Politics,* had been published, and he was returning to the academic world at the age of sixty-five after an absence of thirty-eight years. And he had been instrumental in the election of the first Democratic governor in a Deep South state in over a decade. A couple of real estate transactions had also freed us from some financial burdens.

I felt a twinge as I contemplated my own professional performance over the previous year. I could not identify any one particular achievement. I was grateful that The Jeremiah Project (the creative arts program I directed) had a successful year, and I had worked to expand the reach of my blog. But no particular achievement stood out in my mind. Then it dawned on me—I had devoted major chunks of the year to mothering. While my children are quite grown up, they nevertheless still required mothering. And, like many Lady Boomers I know, I'd donned my Supermom suit, saluted, and rushed to their aid.

The year had been a blur of:

- Airline flights
- Telephone time/FaceTime
- Car travel
- Babysitting
- Economic support
- And so much love

I wouldn't have traded a minute of the time I was lucky enough to spend with my kids and grandchildren. I love them completely. But nearly every time my kids/grandkids call or FaceTime, I drop everything to respond. Not only do I allow a meeting, Zoom session, or doctor's visit to be interrupted, I also permit myself to be pulled away from my passions. I love writing. Writing this book has been the hardest, most fulfilling personal endeavor I've ever undertaken. But I was constantly derailed by the needs of my kids.

Note to self:

BBLB Manual of Maxims #10:
"Don't let kid demands derail the pursuit of your passions."

BBLB RECAP

For many of us, our tenure as moms began in a pickle. Our mother figures established a standard for how to behave as moms while simultaneously projecting their own thwarted ambitions upon us. The outcome? A lot of guilt as we struggled to balance work life with childrearing. From the get-go, guilt robbed us of our jewel tones.

The depletion of key resources (time and money) came at a price: the erosion of our colorful spirits. But recognizing some of our enabling behavior patterns helps reverse the effects of that erosion. Knowledge is liberating and gives us back our power. I have no doubt we will continue to dust off our Super Mom suits when required. But at least ask yourself, "For whom am I doing this? Am I doing my adult child any favors by enabling him/her? Am I exhausting my resources? When am I going to focus on what *I* want? Self-awareness introduces color back into lives turned beige from too many obligations and expectations.

EXERCISE YOUR CREATIVITY #2:

TELL YOUR STORY IN SIX WORDS

Six-word stories are a two-for-one exercise that not only fosters creativity but also helps develop self-awareness. Legend has it Ernest Hemingway originated this genre of storytelling with the line, "For Sale, Baby Shoes, Never Worn." Hemingway's "Baby Shoes" continues to intrigue literary fans to this day, and six-word stories (classified as "short, short stories" or sometimes called "flash fiction") can be found in many libraries and bookstores.

Six-word stories are the perfect little drive-by of emotional expression. It is surprisingly revealing what you can learn from crafting a story out of so few words. The constraint of choosing only six words is freeing. It relieves the pressure of writing a perfect and precise story. The key to the six-word story is finding the best six words to communicate your point.

Examples of six-word stories:
- Conversations about moms make me cry.
- I met my soulmate. He didn't.
- Yesterday, I was a different person.
- Goodbye to you. Hello to me.
- You judge everyone. Am I included?

Spend twenty minutes writing your own six-word story about your experience with mothering—your relationship with your mom or your own mothering memories. You can also write a six-word story focusing on a funny observation about someone else's mothering behavior. Prompts are a great way to prime your writing pump. The following are a few writing prompts for you to ponder:

• A story about advice your mother gave you
• A story about taking your eighteen-year-old to college
• A story about the day you told your children you were divorcing their father
• A story about your favorite family vacation moment
• A story about the mom you noticed in the grocery store

This concise literary genre can help you navigate an array of emotional issues. Use it to capture anxiety, joy, even pain in a succinct way. Playing with the six-word story technique has brought about clarity and relief when I've navigated my own set of stresses. The operative word here is "play." There are no rules. These are exercises by and for yourself and can be shared or not. Discover how fun writing can actually be.

CHAPTER 3:

Brother Time and Sister Space: Navigating Life's Transitions

"When I was alive . . .I said 1:00 as though I could see it, and
"Monday" as though I could find it on a map."
—PETER BEAGLE, *THE LAST UNICORN*

Peter Beagle's allegory begs us to reimagine our concept of time. We regard time as a God, and we are its flock of submissive followers. We worship at the feet of time, creating golden idols in the form of clocks and watches. As one birthday disappears into another, we become preoccupied with the scarcity of time. Lady Boomers are plagued by nagging questions such as, *Am I running out of time? What will the next chapter look like? How much time do I have left?* Time is the magic carpet delivering us from one transition to the next. The only way to suspend the onslaught of time is by fully inhabiting and experiencing the transition, with all the warts and worries accompanying it. That is truly living.

According to Albert Einstein's theory of relativity, time and space are dimensions of the time-space continuum. I picture the two dimensions as members of the same family, a sibling rivalry between time and his sister space.

Time is bossy and hijacks his sister's free spirit. "If it weren't for me, nothing would get done," he accuses. "You would just sit around eating gummies and staring at a lava lamp if I didn't tell you what to do and where to be."

"That is so not true," Space replies. "When I'm fully myself, I notice the hopscotch patterns of light skipping across the grass or the heron hunting for lunch in the bog. It's magical. It's *being* not *doing*. You demand we always be in motion. You are so linear. You constantly think either about the past or what will happen in the future. You refuse to sit within the space of the present, which, my dear brother, is the meaning of life."

"It's my job to allocate space," Time counters. "I provide happy hours, holidays, and weekends for fun and relaxation. But Monday through Friday is the time for punctuality and productivity."

"Do you hear yourself?" Space sputters. "The clock on my cell phone and my Apple watch dictates my life! I experience panic attacks if I'm running late for an appointment. My anxiety knocks me out of the present and makes me so cranky my sense of space is screwed."

"There would be anarchy if I wasn't in charge!" Time retorts.

It feels as though Time holds Space hostage in this endless tug of war. And we tend to acquiesce to this force when in fact we do have a measure of personal control. As Sister Space argued, "We can sit within the space of the present moment." Should we choose to do so, our minutes and hours will elongate, putting us back in the driver's seat of the transition.

My daughter and I share a secret expression. "Mom," she'll say, "I took the time to feel my hands today." Translated: Tracy gave herself permission to experience the surrounding space, undistracted by obligations and responsibilities. I envy her those moments. It's such a relief, like unfastening a bra and throwing it on the floor upon returning home from an obligatory meeting. "*Ahhhh*," the sighs escape from deep within my solar plexus. It's on those occasions we take the time to "ponder a blade of summer grass," as recommended by self-professed lounger and poet, Walt Whitman. There are terms for this kind of respite. "Being present." "Being mindful." "The art of a wasted day," when your soul sneaks up to whisper in your ear.

Inevitably, we will face health transitions, marital and sexual transitions, fashion transitions, even restaurant transitions. How we occupy the space of these transitions determines whether our lives will be enriched by them or diminished.

WHEN DID WE GET SO OLD?

Transitions occur along a linear timeline—childhood, school and college days, work life, child-rearing years, empty nesting, and cresting or crashing into semi-retirement. Perhaps because it was too abstract, the one transition for which boomers failed to plan for—or even face—was aging.

"When did we get so old?" is a question posed by Michele Willens in a 2014 opinion piece in the *New York Times*.

The baby boomer generation, born between 1946 and 1964, has physical concerns: Friends are dying, joints are aching, and memories are failing. There are financial issues, with forced retirement and unemployment, children needing money and possibly a bed, and dependent parents. But for many of us, it is a psychological quandary that is causing the most unpleasantness: looking around and suddenly being the oldest person in the room.[1]

Wait a minute! We used to make fun of old people. "Don't trust anyone over thirty" was a refrain of our generation. It was insinuated we would be forever young. But it appears that Father Time and Mother Nature had other plans for us. At least we're not suffering in silence because there are almost 80 million boomers in the United States.

How do we cope with these time passages? By being fully present in them. To affect the quality of our transitions is the highest of arts.

I look back at significant periods of my life, like when I worked for ten years in a 1920s Spanish-style house in downtown Orlando and conducted survey research for political candidates and environmental groups. Even though I was self-employed, time was my boss. That era I spent traveling to and fro, analyzing data, meeting with clients, and providing space for children on summer breaks consumed my time. And then that time evaporated, leaving behind wisps of memories and forgotten colleagues. Even my home of thirty-two years, which housed newborn babies and a second marriage, is a bygone era of playdates, holiday dinners, and homework hell. I've transitioned to a new home more aptly suited for this time in my life.

Aside from time's status as a god and a boss, Time is also a practical joker with a macabre sense of humor. When we were younger, parenting and work responsibilities robbed us of time for self-nurturing. Now that we have extra hours available to us in retirement or semi-retirement, time taunts us. "Here is more time, but your minutes and hours are numbered." It's hard to win in this time-space relationship.

BBLB Manual of Maxims #11:
"Don't let time be your boss." Take control of
the quality of your days.

COVID-19: THE METAPHORICAL COMMA

COVID-19 failed to provide any kind of transition from our hurried routines to unhurried ones. The big Covid plane in the sky hit the brakes, and the world came to a screeching halt in March 2020. Most transitions offer a little longer runway. Covid was an exceedingly harsh teacher for some, but the virus taught us a lesson about time. I was able to work on this book from my privileged perch, sheltering in place at home. Stories trickled into my world, describing the pervasive problems plaguing families. How to pay the rent or mortgage and utilities? How to work and homeschool children?

Simultaneously, it felt as if there was a paradigm shift challenging our concept of time. We were given a giant pause from our typical frenzied routines, and I began thinking about how best to use that metaphorical comma. Sister Space relished achieving dominion over brother Time during this pause.

Many of my friends and I became increasingly intolerant of schedules as our over-developed sense of responsibility began to relax. We found ourselves repeating a similar refrain:

I can't go to Mount Dora to visit Aunt Mary and her grandchildren? Oh well, maybe some other time. I can't go to my nonprofit office? Oh well, I'll work at home in my pajamas. We can't pay $25 to see a movie? Oh well, I can rent one at home for $5.99 and stop and start it whenever I like. I can't leave my house two hours early to stand in a mile long TSA line, be strip searched, and have my water bottle confiscated in order to fly to Chicago? Oh well, I'll FaceTime with my family and send Easter presents.

"Oh, well" became a new friend and refrain. I'm hoping this new friend accompanies me as I continue to reflect on what's next. I imagine you might feel the same way.

OUTTASIGHT OR OUT OF SIGHT?

Remember the '60s? The 1960s, that is, when "outtasight" referenced something cool and hip? In the '60s, that "something" could have been us baby boomer teen girls. Now we're well into our seventh and eighth decades, and hip and cool are rarely words used to characterize us. I most assuredly fall into this age demographic and a pre-Covid travel experience convinced me we have gone from being "outtasight" to just plain "out of sight."

The trip was to New York City with four other similarly aged women. The entire experience prompted me to ponder how the passage of time has impacted the societal status of Lady Boomers. On one hand, baby boomer women are nearly 40 million strong and enjoy much focus from the media, marketers, and merchants. On the other hand, we tend to be invisible. I am the oldest among this group of friends that consists of a retired lawyer, retired television anchor, retired pharmacist, and practicing lawyer. However, for the sake of this story, I'm lumping our sixty- to seventy-year-old selves into the same age category.

The first clue I had about our invisibility status was at a stand-up comedy club, Carolines on Broadway. Our table virtually abutted the stage, but it may as well have been situated outside in the hall. The young male comics repeatedly ignored our raised hands and eager shouts, choosing cuter, younger audience volunteers for their act. One "comedian" did acknowledge us at one point: "You all have the same hairstyle. Just like Hillary's!" We were not amused.

There were other clues pointing to our Casper the Ghost status—i.e., cab drivers ignoring our hails and ticket takers our stubs. Now, I realize we were visiting a fast-paced urban city, but more than once a fast-paced professional crashed into one of us, reacting with irritated surprise that we were even occupying sidewalk real estate in front of him.

On the other hand, there were and are some advantages to this status. Our age and various infirmities enabled us to jump the queue in the forty-five-minute line to enter the 9/11 museum, a big help given the cold wind and rain. We always had a seat on the subway. Melissa's thirty-one-year tenure as an anchor on the CBS affiliate in Louisville, Kentucky, enabled us to get a tour of the control room and set of the CBS Morning News show. We met Gayle King and her guest star, former Superwoman Lynda Carter. (Now *that* was affirming as the then seventy-seven-year-old former superhero looked great and has an irreverent sense of humor.) Since we are of a certain age, we have connections that enabled us to get backstage access to a Broadway play owing to a daughter's relationship with the female lead. But, by far, my favorite line of the weekend regarding the freedom afforded us by our invisibility was uttered by one of my travel companions: "We could smoke a bong on Fifth Avenue and the police would assume someone else was blowing smoke in our faces." This experience merited two maxims from the *BBLB Manual*.

Remember, *BBLB Manual of Maxims #7:* "Cultivate a sense of humor"; it will come in handy as you navigate aging transitions.

BBLB Manual of Maxims #12:
"Hold your friends dear." The camaraderie, laughter, and shared understanding of our passages helps preserve and restore our color.

WHAT'S THE BEST RESTAURANT OVER FIFTY? HOME, APPARENTLY.

Even though parts of us are fading, and we seem to be disappearing into invisibility, eating at familiar restaurants where they know your name and it's quiet enough to hear your companions speak is a great way to offset the invisibility slights.

My friend Stan is a connoisseur of fine dining establishments. (He is also a connoisseur of fine wine and Scotch, a hobby enjoyed by people who have the luxury of time sans kids.) As much as we enjoy eating, my husband and I are not hip to the newest and coolest restaurants. We rely on Stan (who lives three hundred miles away) to up our cool quotient on the restaurant front. In our own backyards we frequent our four or five favs. They are comfortable. The proprietors recognize us. We can hear ourselves talk. Our taste buds anticipate our two or three favorite dishes. In short, we have become Culinary Curmudgeons, as Frank Bruni refers to himself.

In his 2019 article entitled, "The Best Restaurant If You Are Over 50," Bruni contends:

> *It's not just sex and sleep that change once you get over the age of 50, it's supper! What becomes more important is hearing and really being able to talk with your tablemates rather than trying virgin cuisines.*[2]

Ina Garten, the Barefoot Contessa, says she and her husband go to the same restaurant over and over again until they can't do it anymore. In their seventies, Ina and Jeffrey are "unapologetic creatures of habit." We frequent places that, as Frank Bruni says, ". . . have a bearable din and comfortable chairs" (eschewing those with stools having no lumbar support and those requiring a smart phone flashlight to read the menu).

This meal metamorphosis has resulted in dining at home with friends. Embarrassingly enough, once you get beyond a table of five, it's hard to hear or even engage with party participants in noisy restaurants. My dining table comfortably seats a party of eight. I actually don't even want to host a dinner party larger than eight. Another transition I'm experiencing is the desire to talk in-depth with friends rather than engaging in superficial conversations with multiple people, so food isn't the ultimate objective of these gatherings. It's the fellowship with people I care about. Our relationships are infused with history. It's the relationships that are now more nourishing than the fancy foods of yesteryear.

My friend Ann was bereft following the abrupt closure of a favorite restaurant. Baja Kitchen was an order-at-the-counter kind of place where the upholstery was held together in places by duct tape. But the food was good, and the staff called her by name. "Where will I have lunch on Mondays now?" she wailed.

What is it about these special places? Maybe it's the comfort they provide amid the discomfort of aging. I no longer have the patience to wait sixty minutes or even thirty for a table or to navigate a complicated cocktail menu. I have a few favorite libations, honed over time, to celebrate (or blunt) the end of a day. According to Bruni, the word "restaurant" means to "restore one's spirit." I don't care about perfectly prepared palette pleasers as much as I care to restore my spirit with the comfort of cherished companions.

I overheard a man confronting a hostess at Hillstone Restaurant in Orlando one weekend evening. "Lady, I'm ninety-two, and you are literally subtracting minutes from my life making me wait like this. I don't have extra to spare." While he was obnoxious, I understood his sentiment. I know I've grown increasingly impatient at what I perceive to be lost minutes, too. The gentlemen huffed out of the restaurant ten minutes later. I guess he was opting to be in the driver's seat of his time and life. The way he careened out of the parking lot, however, made me wish he hadn't been in the driver's seat of a real car.

Transitions are like mathematical equations. Convert a minus into a plus and the result is a net neutral. The subtractions don't hurt so much with this attitude.

RETIRED HUSBAND SYNDROME

My husband moved his office into our home when he turned sixty-five. Technological advances have enabled him to operate without the burden of a five-room office condo, copy machine, landlines, or even a receptionist. He confessed to some anxiety about this transition since for years he rose each morning, got dressed, and headed to an office. "Going to the office" had been the thing he'd done more of in his life than literally anything else.

Jim is a great partner and readily participates in household chores. His last name is Kitchens, which is an accurate reflection of how adept he is in ours. The management of the rest of our home, however, is usually my responsibility. Broken disposal, stopped-up toilet, lawn maintenance, and dead electrical sockets generally fall to me or at least to the contact list in my iPhone. I schedule Spectrum, plumbers, and ADT security personnel for home repair visits. But he stepped up and took over the management of some of these tasks once he moved his office into our home and was more available during weekdays.

Most of the women I know are excellent multitaskers. They are adept at performing multiple tasks simultaneously, seemingly without the need to share the specifics of their accomplishments in excruciating detail. The same can't be said for most men I've known. They tend not to suffer their accomplishments, small or large, in silence.

Upon my arrival home from work one afternoon, my husband couldn't wait to share the story of his day, one that frustrated him and amused me. I was greeted with, "Oh my God what a day I've had!" I forced myself not to roll my eyes at the drama infusing this statement, instead saying, "I'm all ears."

That morning, our repairman, Art, had arrived to fix the toilet, garage door, and electrical outlet. As it turned out, he was able to repair everything but the garage door. The spring had broken and would require the expertise of a real garage door repair company. Posthaste, a garage door repairman (and his ten-year-old son) arrived while Jim was in the shower. Jim, soapy hair and all, showed the man to our garage. Minutes later, the man was back with a bathroom request for his son. Our two dogs were bouncing off the walls, barking with excitement as they welcomed the visitors. Twenty minutes later, Gabriel (my husband was now on a first name basis with the garage door repairman) appeared at the back door with a bloody hand. After applying Bactine and Band-Aids, Gabriel was dispatched to an urgent care center for treatment. The dogs went ballistic for a second time when the UPS delivery man dropped off a package, interrupting Jim's attempt at analyzing polling data. The last insult to injury was the Terminix pest control guy showing up for a quarterly treatment. The dogs, once again, played havoc with Jim's conference call.

I was appropriately sympathetic in my response, all the while fighting to keep the corners of my mouth in a neutral position rather than revealing the hilarity I was suppressing. And truly, I understood his pain because I'd been responsible for those tasks for years. Multitasking is hard. As men transition from office/airplane to home, these situations, and the associated drama, will become more commonplace. Just hope they can handle it.

Retired Spouse Syndrome is an actual phenomenon and a major transition for both spouses, according to a 2006 episode of ABC's *Good Morning America*. The syndrome was diagnosed in Japan in 2006 when the first wave of boomer men began retiring. Eighty-five percent of men were excited at the prospect of retiring; 40 percent of women were depressed at the prospect. Women developed stress reactions such as rashes, ulcers, and the desire to toss their spouses out the window.[3] The husband of my friend, Bridget, spent so much post-retirement time on the sofa watching television he needed a hip replacement.

BBLB Manual of Maxims #13:
"Be kind and patient with yourself during major changes."

The lives of working people are totally bricked up by seconds, minutes, and weekends, with little room for flexibility. Redefining time is one of the goals of retirement or semi-retirement. Continuing with the wisdom of Peter Beagle, "We live in houses bricked up with seconds and minutes . . . I never went outside because there was no other door. Now I know that I could have walked through walls." So it's an excellent time to walk through a few walls (try, however, to avoid throwing him/her through one.)

HOW MANY PAIRS OF BLACK PANTS DOES ONE WOMAN NEED?!

It's a rhetorical question: how many pairs of black pants does one woman need?

This question popped into my head when my husband and I were vacationing in Europe one summer. Because we traveled to five different destinations, there were many days I didn't bother to unpack; my suitcase served as my dresser. And quite frankly, my suitcase resembled my dresser at home. Bras intermingled with shirts; shorts mixed up with underwear. No matter how many times I repacked to make access easier, each day I had to rummage through my suitcase because the item I sought was *always* inaccessible. It was during one of these delving days I realized I was the proud possessor of multiple pairs of black pants, from shorts to capris to ankle length trousers. Inevitably I would say, in a decidedly crabby voice, "Not *that* pair of black pants." (Since I shared hotel rooms with my husband, he was the lucky recipient of my cranky clothing rants.)

Traveling is a great opportunity for self-discovery. Were it not for my daily suitcase searches, I doubt I would have realized I owned so many pairs of black pants. (Home closets are good at hiding our clothing transitions.) When and how did that happen? Looking down at the bulge of belly fat hanging over my underwear, I answered my own question. There is obviously a correlation between my weight gain and how much better my stomach and butt look in black. Time is not always kind to women's bodies. Another one of those transition inevitabilities is a slowing metabolism as we age. Even when we put up a good fight, it gets harder to lose weight. So we must be brave enough to readjust.

The readjustment phase can take one of two paths. (1) Obscure the fat folds, or (2) Just say f%$# it. Transition from caring how others regard your generous bosom or chunky hips.

Black pants seem to be a strategy for Path One. I actually think transitioning to black is a resourceful move. Black is slenderizing and can be worn with any kind of colorful top. But outside of black, clothing choices for older, curvy women are limited. In a 2016 *NPR* interview, fashion guru, Tim Gunn calls attention to this fashion crime. He says, "It's a disgrace designers refuse to make clothes to fit American women. Far more women wear a size sixteen than size six, but the industry seems not to have noticed."[4] He indicts fashion designers for their lack of effort in appealing to the 100 million plus-sized women in America. While I love that Tim Gunn had the courage to criticize the fashion industry for this design failure, I don't love the term "plus-sized." That description alone is enough to make us want to say f%$# it to fashion.

I vote for *both* options (obscure the fat folds *and* just say f%$# it). As much as I grumbled about all the black pants I packed for my trip, they offered a great deal of flexibility in mixing and matching. Black's job is also to serve as our accomplice in concealing expanding waistlines (and I think she does a pretty good job of it). And, if the fashion industry is not interested in designing well-fitted clothing for curvy women, then f%$# them. Let's err on the side of comfort. It's time to own and accept our bodies. Once we do, we will truly enjoy the spaciousness of this fashion transition.

Apparently, my computer knows my penchant for black pants because an ad keeps popping up on Facebook for the "little black pant guaranteed to be the best fitting pants you will ever buy." My hand keeps hovering over the "order" button; meanwhile, my husband hovers over me, trying to swat my hand away.

COVID-INSPIRED FASHION LIBERATION

Saying eff it to fashion was a mantra for many women during Covid.

Early on during the pandemic, after wearing the same muumuu for three days straight, I posted the following on Facebook: "I realize this is a minor matter, but if this keeps up I'm going to have to buy more loungewear."

Friends and acquaintances dove into the conversation:

I know. I have to force myself to put on real clothes.

I gave up on real clothes. Stretch pants for days. I stopped by the church today braless and in my fuzzy slippers and it was great!

Why bother with real clothes when we can't go anywhere?

I'm debating the need for a shower today.

This is an opportunity to find out what my real hair color is.

Does lounge wear include pajamas?

Me too! My husband, however, might leave me, as he is tired of the same set three days in a row.

Don't rush the shower—you have all day tomorrow.

The liberation of fashion constraints during Covid was freeing. Many of my friends gave up coloring their hair. Comfortable clothes became a must. Who needed lipstick and blush when a mask obscured your face? I think many of these shifts in our behaviors will remain. The pandemic taught us we like being comfortable and unpainted.

Speaking of our generation, we were the girls in the Women's Liberation Movement, fighting for greater personal freedom. The movement campaigned for equal pay, access to better health care and birth control, and more educational opportunities. We also burned our bras to symbolize throwing away things that oppressed and confined us. Frankly, I don't know why we ever decided to take them out of the incinerators. The pandemic gave almost every woman I know a free pass to go braless. Confined to our homes, why in the world would we consider confining our breasts?

ONE OF MY FAVORITE ESSAYS from 2020 was titled "A Letter from the Contents of My Bra Drawer," by Elizabeth Yuko:

Dear Elizabeth, we wanted to check in. Is everything OK? It's been a few weeks since we last saw you and we're getting worried. It was on a Monday. You'd showered—a vanishingly rare event these days—and put on pants with a button. What's going on? Have you given up on wearing bras completely? Look, we know we're not your favorite garment. You made that abundantly clear each time you unhooked us and threw us on the floor the minute you got home from work. But honestly, we miss you. We miss the smell of your deodorant and getting to feel the fresh air when our straps have the opportunity to peek out from under your shirt—even if only for a few minutes. A bra is only as good as the last time it propped up a bosom. For us, that last time is a distant memory.[5]

My mother told me never to leave the house without looking presentable (bra, lipstick, neatly coiffed hair.) And that mom-mandate stayed with me—until now.

BBLB Manual of Maxims #14:
"Allow comfort to govern your fashion choices."

VIKING: THE CRUISE WHERE ROMANCE GOES TO DIE

It's ironic that when we finally have the time and space to engage in romantic frivolities, time has played havoc with our bodies and desires.

My husband and I have traveled on a couple of Viking cruises over the past few years (all pre-Covid), and during our most recent trip I observed—over the course of eight days—an amalgamation of mostly American, mostly white, married and single sixty-plus-year-olds. It's not often I'm in a position to encounter such a homogenous slice of the population in one space. And for someone in the research biz, this phenomenon offered too tantalizing an independent study to pass up. One conclusion? I'm surprised one of Viking's competitors hasn't come up with some version of the following marketing message:

"Looking for romance? Well, you won't find it on a Viking cruise. Instead, sail with us on Celebrity, Carnival, Royal Caribbean . . ."

My husband and I were perched on the ship's pool deck one afternoon, people-watching. We observed that men congregated with men and women with women. It didn't look like an environment conducive to hooking up for singles or married couples. And I have to say, I put the blame squarely on the men. Even my husband agreed.

Not being an avid sunbather at plus-fifty-five residential communities, I failed to realize how few parents in the 1940s and '50s properly instructed their sons on how to avoid "manspreading." For the uninitiated (count me among the previously uninitiated) manspreading is the practice whereby a man adopts a seated (or semi-reclined) position with his legs spread apart. Apparently, the practice has been banned in Madrid since it takes up too many seats on public transportation. I think it also needs to be banned while wearing a bathing suit in a public area. These guys were splayed out spread eagle on deck chairs. Did they really think those little net jobs cover much? I constantly had to avert my eyes. I feel a great deal of love and loyalty to a certain man's aging balls, but not to all the rest of them. Even though my husband has manners enough not to engage in this sitting behavior, it was such a romantic buzz kill that I wasn't in the mood for hooking up even with him.

Girls of my generation were coached, even nagged, to "always keep your knees together." "Be ladylike when you're sitting." "Keep your thighs, knees, and ankles in constant contact." Obviously, boys didn't receive the same memo.

In case I required another lesson in older men's immodesty, I observed a roughly eighty-five-year-old man as he staggered into the atrium bar/coffee shop wearing only the requisite white terry-cloth robe provided by the ship (to be worn *only* in the spa, stateroom, or pool deck.) He was clutching his clothes, including the tighty whities I saw him retrieve from the floor en route from the spa. Sidling up to the bar, he began talking loudly to the female bartender. "You're from the Philippines, right? I love Filipinos. One took care of me after my surgery." I don't think he was hitting on her, but I noticed a couple of women nearby roll their eyes.

I'm probably not going to contact Celebrity or Carnival cruise lines with my marketing advice. I doubt Viking is the only cruise line that caters to our age demographic and creates a romance-killing shipboard culture.

BBLB Manual of Maxims #15:
"Don't be an entitled old person."

At the very least, it's not attractive and kills the urge for romance. And romance, at whatever age, is important and revitalizing. It gives us a sense of lightness and buoyancy, making these time transitions a lot more bearable.

I NEED PEPTO AND PERRIER!

My husband and I visited our friend, Stan, the fine dining aficionado mentioned earlier, in his hometown of Miami. Stan planned a culinary evening for us at the Bazaar Mar, a restaurant owned by James Beard Award-winning chef, Jose Andres. Andres's 2018 book, *We Fed an Island,* had just been released.[6] The book describes the eighteen kitchens he set up all over the island of Puerto Rico following the devastation of Hurricane Maria. During his three-month tenure on his native island, they served over three million meals. His Michelin star restaurants, like the one we were visiting, help fund his philanthropy.

Our meal at his Miami restaurant consisted of course after course of small plates, each with excruciating flavor profiles (my vocabulary does not house such descriptors. "Excruciating flavor profiles" lives in Stan's world, not mine.). Every fifteen minutes during our four-hour gastro experience, waiters deposited delicacies such as an Asian taco on a kale chip with yellow tail tuna and caviar, and the tiniest sugar cone filled with salmon mousse. The choreography and precision of their presentations (which included hand flourishes) were as enjoyable as the food.

"How do you feel about sparklers?" Stan asked early in the evening, and right then, as if he was David Copperfield, the wine steward magically produced a bottle of icy brut champagne. There was also a white blend of seven, eight, or nine grapes, rounding out our alcohol consumption. (Oh, did I mention we first met in the bar for cocktails featuring concoctions such as a "salt air" foamed margarita?)

A deconstructed key lime pie, shaved grapefruit ice, and the requisite chocolate souffle put an end to our food intake. Fortunately, our Aloft Hotel was a few blocks away, providing a way for our bodies to move around a few of the three thousand calories we had just ingested. As we walked, I saw a neon green "P" flashing like a beacon. "It's a Publix!" I cheered. "I can get some Pepto-Bismol and Perrier!" These are my go-to remedies for indigestion, and my sixty-five-year-old body was in dire need of relief.

Twenty-six years earlier, when I was thirty-nine, my husband and I enjoyed a gastro tour of Miami, also guided by Stan. We lunched at Joe's Stone Crab, enjoyed Flamenco dancing at a Cuban restaurant on Calle Ocho (eighth street), and dined at the Intercontinental to the accompaniment of a South American harpist. It was truly an eat-a-palooza. I fared much better at thirty-nine, however, than I did at sixty-five. This more recent food-fest reminded me of how much my body and pocketbook had transitioned beyond this extravagant drinking and dining lifestyle. Those twenty-six extra birthdays had diminished my digestive tract's ability to ingest with abandon. But the experience was fun and delicious. The minutes and hours felt elongated that evening and boy, did I take time to enjoy the surrounding space.

BBLB RECAP

Transitions are inevitable, and how we choose to navigate these passages makes us the bosses of our minutes and hours. Our nests may have been violated as our spouses retire and take up more real estate. For many of us, our ears, wallets, and stomachs can no longer tolerate noisy restaurants and rich foods. Travel requires more planning, and who in the hell replaced our short skirts with too many pairs of black pants?! Fear often causes us to erect barriers to ward off change, walling us off from our truth. Rather than dreading or fretting about these transitions, why not handle them as Peter Beagle suggested? Try walking through a few of Time's walls.

BBLB Manual of Maxims #16:
"Don't worship at the feet of Brother Time. Pay homage to Sister Space."

Doing so guarantees you will find your sassy self.

EXERCISE YOUR CREATIVITY #3:

CREATE YOUR OWN TIME PIE

I have read books, listened to podcasts, and watched TED talks about finding balance. For many, life balance equals personal happiness. But I've concluded that, for me, achieving a consistent balance is a myth. It's just one more thing to add to my to-do lists. It adds pressure and a sense of failure if we don't achieve the goal.

I do, however, believe in self-awareness. Recognizing how we spend our minutes and hours can be illuminating. Effecting the quality of our days is a worthy goal and the point of this chapter.

Spend twenty minutes creating your Time Pie. On a blank piece of paper, draw a large circle representing your life. On a separate piece of paper, write down categories reflecting how you spend your time. Below is a list of potential categories and colors. Feel free to edit the categories and the colors to more aptly fit your life. Use crayons, paints, or colored pencils to fill in the categories of your life. Add more of each of the colors representing areas where you spend the most time; add fewer of the colors where you spend the least amount of time. If you like, you can even assign your favorite colors to areas of your life you enjoy the most and your least favorite colors for time spent on activities you enjoy the least. Now take a dark pen or marker and segment the categories. The lines can be curvy, or you can use a ruler to help slice your pie.

Turquoise–Social: Visiting friends and acquaintances, dining out, attending cultural/sporting events

Violet–Spiritual: Attending religious services, meditating, studying sacred text

Yellow–Family: Caring for family members, visiting/calling/FaceTiming with family

Red–Work: Paid and unpaid activities involving structured time, including volunteering and activities with income potential

Green–Health: Medical appointments, therapy sessions, exercise, nutrition

Tangerine–Hobbies/interests: Reading, sewing, woodworking, puzzling, music and/or visual arts, journaling, watching Netflix/television, browsing the Web

Burnt Umber–Home Maintenance: Cleaning, yard work, routine cooking

Cobalt Blue–Travel: Vacationing, day trips (I would put trips to visit family members in the family category as they aren't always as relaxing as vacation getaways)

I find that visual illustrations provide clarity. Step back and assess your time. Are you happy with the distribution of your time? Do you find you're spending more time performing tasks you find unfulfilling? How might you adjust? How can you take back the reins of your own time?

CHAPTER 4:

Your Rx for Aging

"Breakin' Up Is Hard to Do."
—NEIL SEDAKA

Just what is the prescription for aging? Ponce de Leon wasn't the only one in pursuit of the Fountain of Youth. The dread of aging is the fear the grim reaper is coming to take away not just our souls but also our physical and mental abilities. Even short of dire diagnoses, breaking up with formerly functioning body parts is hard to do. Is it possible to delay deterioration?

There are people, known as Superagers, who seem to be able to turn back their biological clocks, living like fifty-year-olds well into their eighties thanks to strenuous exercise and eating in color. But even those of us who don't fall into the Superager category can play like we're police and arrest aging even a bit by taking baby steps toward modest health goals.

There is an inevitability to aches and pains, but how we confront these weaknesses is the real story of our later years. I never imagined I'd become a person to go on and on about my myriad maladies—broken wrist, joint replacements, foot drop, never ending hot flashes—but I became that person. Karma paid me back for all the times I rolled my eyes when my father-in-law complained about his infirmities in excruciating detail. How we choose to navigate our physical transitions makes us the boss of the process. BBLB encourages all of us ornery oldsters to whip out our 1960s protest buttons and say no to the beige rules and expectations associated with aging. That is my Rx for Aging.

BREAKING UP IS HARD TO DO

Playing Euchre (a four-person card game originating in the Midwest) with friends one night in 2019, I detailed various surgeries I'd undergone over the previous fifteen years. I counted twelve. All had been successful, to the point that I had become cavalier about the surgical process.

"Oh, it's nothing," I would say to friends. "I plan to have all my body parts replaced." Well, the surgery count subsequently increased to fourteen following knee-replacement surgery and an operation installing hardware in my fractured wrist. I'm here to attest, breaking up with functioning body parts is hard to do.

My initial carefree attitude toward surgery came back to haunt me when I awoke from my knee-replacement surgery with a drop foot on the same leg.

"This is extremely rare," observed my orthopedic surgeon. "I kept the tourniquet on for only twenty-three minutes."

Tourniquet?!

I realized how little I knew about this process. Once

again, my jaunty mindset hadn't prompted me to question the doctor about the process.

I was told nerves heal quite slowly. I wore a brace in my shoe to keep my toes elevated in order to avoid tripping and landing on my newly renovated knee, and my floppy foot proved to be a source of annoyance, anxiety, and humility. I panicked about not being able to do the things I'd hoped to be able to do following the installation of my bionic knee: bike riding, hiking, golfing, walking. I couldn't drive, so I was forced to rely on others. Therein lies the real rub. I love my independence, and I don't want people knowing where I am at all moments of the day. I love spontaneously hopping on my bike and riding to the grocery store. But after five months of physical therapy (two days each week with a few acupuncture treatments thrown in for good measure) I was ready to roll. I felt normal again, returning to my daily rituals and routines. I could drive again. I could ride my e-bike again. Hallelujah! The control-a-holic in me was euphoric. For a while, anyway.

Then a fateful Sunday crushed my short-lived euphoria. Fall had finally fallen in Florida after what felt like an endless summer of ninety-plus-degree days.

"Let's ride our bikes to church," I begged my husband. My kind husband finds it hard to say no to me (or possibly doesn't want to endure my whining and pleading), so off we careened to Knowles Chapel, about six miles from our home. "Careen" is the operative word, as it turned out. I had a particular route in mind, my husband another. The upshot? Our careening resulted in a collision in which I served as the cushion for my husband's fall. There was such a clatter that neighbors sprang from their beds to see what was the matter. The matter turned out to be a fractured wrist and ankle (*of course* the ankle attached to the drop foot) and road rash from skidding across the asphalt. My husband walked away unscathed, but repairing my wrecked wrist required a metal plate and multiple screws.

Thus began life with my left hand. I saw the movie *My Left Foot* when it was first released. I think there should be a sequel called *My Left Hand* to document the hilarity and humility of having the use of only one's left hand. I have read that left-hand dominant people tend to have faster connections between the right and left hemispheres of the brain, which leads to quicker information processing. I am so right-hand dominant I wonder if the hemispheres of my brain communicate at all. Adjusting to life with only one hand (the other being wrapped from elbow to knuckles) and barely two feet proved beyond challenging. My shirts sustained permanent stains from food dropped from the fumbled fork. Oh, and the indignities! Like fastening a bra. Pouring sixty-seven-year-old boobs into a bra in front of an audience (the audience being my husband whose hands were required to fasten the hooks) was humbling, to say the least. Sponge baths were necessary in the early days following surgery. My husband lingered nearby, fearing I might fall and hurt myself—not an irrational fear considering my past year. Ordinarily, bath time includes clothes and towels to help obscure flab and folds. But not during bath time standing under LED lights above the kitchen sink. A friend confided that pursuant to a severely broken leg, her mate had to lift her on and off the toilet. Now *that* puts intimacy to a real test.

Texting, my favorite mode of communication, proved difficult with only one available thumb. Friends and family were enlisted to cut my food into bite-sized portions. Driving was banned, triggering my aforementioned control issues again. But vanity dominated as my chief complaint. "How can I fix my hair with only one hand?" I wailed. Hair renders women vulnerable, especially as we age and our hair loses body and density. Coiffing demands multiple hands. The blow dryer goes in one hand, the brush in the other. Simple, except when you only have one hand!

Breaking up with functioning body parts can catapult you into a dark place. I don't think I had been sufficiently empathetic with people about the psychic results of an injury or health issue. The panic. The depression. It's easy to pull in, tending to your wounds, not wanting to put on a happy face. As Joni Mitchell sang, "Don't it always seem to go that you don't know what you've got 'til it's gone?"

But a funny thing happens when you have really good friends and family members. They keep reaching in and pulling you out of the quicksand of self-pity. They start by bringing over food. Then they drive you places—physical therapy, lunch, shopping. Then they have faith when you lose yours. Then they remind you of the things you enjoy in your life. "Come ride with me in my golf cart. You can drive the cart. You can chip and putt." Obviously, the diminished nerve in my foot managed to travel up to my brain, diminishing my memories of what made me happy.

There were also a few silver linings. Prior to my injuries, visits to a hair salon were restricted to once every six weeks. I bought a package of eight "blow outs" and visited the salon once a week, improving my self-image exponentially.

("Wow, your hair looks really good" was a comment I heard frequently from friends and acquaintances. "Don't get used to it," I would reply.) I couldn't cook for fear of injuring my one remaining good hand. Since my injury and surgery occurred late in November, Thanksgiving dinner preparations were out of the question. Oh darn. Thanksgiving is not my favorite holiday or meal. There are just too many expectations. Oh, and I finally learned to dictate text messages and Google questions using the microphone feature on my iPhone.

It is inevitable that we, or those we love, will experience illnesses or injuries during our BBLB years. So just as we must be the boss of time, we also have to be the boss of our attitudes. I could cite five maxims from the *BBLB Manual* on this topic, but I'll stick to two.

BLB Manual of Maxims #17:
"Seek out the silver linings."

I know it sounds Pollyanna, but this is an essential commandment. There are opportunities woven into the fabric of every predicament. They will help you avoid slipping into beigedom and perhaps provide a new sense of purpose.

Remember, *BLB Manual of Maxims* #12: "Hold your friends dear." You are going to need them in your BBLB injury-prone years.

EATING IN COLOR

A friend told me she was committed to losing weight via Weight Watchers. With more than a little grousing and grumbling, she recorded each morsel that made its way into her mouth. (At least the current Weight Watchers program isn't as grueling as earlier versions that required weighing everything you ingested.) With this new version, every step my friend took, every move she made, was tracked via Weight Watchers e-tools. (Listening to Lisa, I was tempted to break out singing the Police's hit, "Every Breath You Take," but since she was complaining, it felt inappropriate.) The WW program offers great incentive to garner activity points. Extra activity points mean extra food (and alcohol). Slowly, steadily, she shed pounds.

My friend Billy lost thirty-five pounds through a similar dieting strategy. Billy talked about eating more mindfully, paying attention, and appreciating each forkful of food. He said that grabbing a bag of chips had been his afternoon MO prior to entering the world of weight loss. Now, he would substitute an apple or orange; the ritual of slicing the fruit and its visual impact on the plate actually appealed to him.

Ok, so I gave in and decided to address my widening waistline. I attended motivational lectures with titles like "Snacking Smarter" and "Produce Power." During my first visit, the meeting leader distributed a brochure urging participants to "color up your plate." The color comes from orange carrots, red peppers, and green leafy lettuces. All this rich, beautiful "color" costs the dieter 0 food points in the Weight Watchers World.

The coaches had me at "color up your plate." Color is obviously a defining characteristic of *Be Brave. Lose the*

Beige! It conveys creative thinking. Hopefully, by now you have tried at least one of the "Exercise Your Creativity" tasks sprinkled throughout this book. Exercising your creative muscles helps you think creatively about other aspects of your life. And yes, that includes dieting. Typical dieting strategies are boring and require sacrifice, and Lady Boomers are sick to death of sacrifice. So how can we "color up" a mundane task such as dieting? I subscribed to *Cooking Light* magazine. I liked the menu makeovers for grilling healthy burgers. I enjoyed trying obscure recipes such as the Indonesian vegetable salad. I actually found the process interesting; it appealed to my creative spirit. So whether it's dieting or some other potentially dreaded endeavor, approaching it with a spirit of mindfulness and creativity will make the endeavor not only more bearable but even fun and life-enriching.

SUPERAGERS ARE SUPER PEOPLE

I don't think in all good conscience I can issue aging prescriptions without mentioning the F-word. No, guess again. This F-word is not about sex or swearing. It stands for Fitness. Lisa Feldman Barrett, in a 2016 *New York Times* article, outlined the criteria for becoming a "Superager":

> *Why do some older people remain mentally nimble while others decline? Superagers are those whose memory is actually on a par with healthy, active 25-year-olds.*[1]

As mentally nimble as a twenty-five-year-old? That claim seemed far-fetched. Apparently, though, research suggests that working hard at something increases the chance of remaining mentally sharp even as we venture into the last trimester of our lives. There are critical regions of our brains that remain thick and healthy through vigorous exercise or disciplined mental efforts. And these researchers aren't talking just about playing Candy Crush online or even doing crossword puzzles. They're referring to the kind of mental exercise called for when learning a new language or a musical instrument.

According to the article, Superagers are the Marines of maturing adults. Not only do their workout routines have to be difficult, there must also be an element of discomfort from the exertion, which builds muscles and mental discipline. (I'm sure this description alone has you creeping back to the sofa to binge-watch the latest season of *The Great British Baking Show* while stuffing your mouth with Paul Hollywood's hot cross buns.)

This Superager article reminded me of the book, *Younger Next Year,* wherein author Chris Crowley maintains that the ticket to turning back the biological clock and living like fifty-year-olds well into our eighties is strenuous exercise–the spin class workout or power yoga kind of exercise. Superagers excel at pushing past the temporary unpleasantness of intense effort.

It is human nature to avoid unpleasantness. As we age, though, this tendency becomes more acute as we sidestep situations that make us uncomfortable. It would be so easy to sidestep challenging physical or mental exertions. We feel we've earned the right to relax and take it easy. But no, we need these exertions now more than ever. Even if you're tempted to say *eff it* to strenuous physical or mental exertion, try taking a baby step, even in the form of buying a Fitbit and tracking your steps. You don't want to risk succumbing to the adage, "If you don't use it, you lose it."

AGEIST ATTITUDES TOWARD ATHLETICISM

Hearing the description of Superagers could easily conjure up images of athletes dunking basketballs or hitting home runs. "In order to be capable of engaging in strenuous exercise, you must be athletic," is an excuse I've heard for avoiding swimming laborious laps or doing arduous abs workouts. So, who, in fact, does "count" as an athlete? A couple of fitness gurus I queried suggested: "A person trained or gifted in exercises or contests involving physical agility, stamina, or strength; a participant in a sport, exercise, or game requiring physical skill."

Societal expectations set the bar pretty high. Talent, special gifts, agility, and skill seem to be prerequisites for the designation. Since Boomers have a history of defying norms and expectations, I don't think we should stop now. I propose a new definition:

> *An athlete is someone who is committed to fitness and/or physical activity. These people are brave and don't accept limitations. They find workarounds when physical injuries or other circumstances interfere with performance abilities. When faced with obstacles, they choose an adjacent path. They don't give up.*

Body parts wear out and often need repairing or replacing. But that fact doesn't preclude exercise. My definition of an athlete is someone who makes exercise a priority and refuses to be defeated by infirmities. "Ok, so my bum knee interferes with walking and biking. I can still lift weights or swim."

I became increasingly aware of ageist attitudes related to athleticism during my spate of injuries. Admittedly, for a while I looked like a mummy in my wrapped wrist and casted ankle. Threading my way through strangers in Starbucks one morning, I realized I was avoiding eye contact, unwilling to endure the sympathy in other people's glances as I hobbled around in my boot. I strongly suspect if I had been forty-six rather than sixty-six, the looks might have been replete with empathy or even admiration. If you're forty-six and in a cast, the default assumption is that of course you're going to get back on the horse; if you're sixty-six, you might as well just sell the damn horse. I had every intention of getting back on my bike (even though my friends kept threatening to envelop me in bubble wrap if I did). But that isn't living. Movement is an essential component of being alive. "Real" athletes don't want to just sit on the sofa watching other athletes. They want to participate.

I've taken creative liberties with my revised definition of athleticism. Defying and redefining social norms is the point of this book. Just because we may not be gifted at dunking a basketball or throwing a curve ball doesn't mean we aren't athletes.

BBLB Manual of Maxims #18:
"Be brave. Don't accept physical limitations. Invent your own definition of athleticism."

That's your creative choice.

GOD'S GYMNASIUM

A sense of place is important to promote and encourage physical and mental wellness. My own fitness journey has taken me to the Center for Health and Wellbeing, located in Winter Park, Florida. Designers of this center intentionally chose the term "wellbeing" rather than "wellness" because their focus is broader, emphasizing the mind and spirit as well as the physical aspect of fitness. I like this comprehensive approach and the fact the center is conveniently located. It's a ten minute drive from my home (twenty-three minutes by bicycle) so I don't have to burn too many calories getting there. I believe this sense of place can be achieved in other venues. Just being outside walking, biking, or swimming in God's gorgeous gymnasium facilitates that same sense of place.

When I turned sixty, I gave myself a gift by attending a positive aging conference in Sarasota, Florida (an epicenter for older adults). Since I was segueing into my later years, I wanted tips on navigating this transition. One session was entitled, "Sitting is the New Smoking." While researchers for the *American Journal of Public Health* dispute this notion, they did note that excessive sitting increases the risk of premature death and chronic illnesses.[2] My takeaway? Get off the sofa! A commitment to fitness, in whatever form, takes a measure of bravery. Workouts are hard, but they help ward off the grim reaper.

SENIOR MOMENT, OR OOPS, I FORGOT WHAT I WAS GOING TO SAY

Considering our age, I'm assuming most will recognize the term "senior moment," the definition of which is "a temporary mental lapse, humorously attributed to the gradual loss of one's mental faculties as one grows older." (At least we hope and pray these are temporary lapses.)

My friend Suzi refers to such lapses as her "blonde moments." Regardless of the label, I had one such lapse as I excitedly prepared to play golf with friends. "Prepare" is the operative word here. There are the golf clothes, golf shoes, golf socks, and golf hat to don. Do I have enough balls and tees in my bag? Since golfing takes an inordinate amount of the day, I had to make sure the dogs were walked so they wouldn't leave unappreciated deposits in the house in my absence. Of course, that meant taking the poop bags to the garbage after the walk. So while I was hanging out by the garbage in the garage, I decided, for efficiency's sake, to move my clubs into the alley behind the garage for easier pickup. My car was parked in front of our townhouse. Between the time I reentered my house and hopped in my car, being the crazed multitasker that I am, I decided to run the dishwasher and answer a text.

Wait for it—here it comes. I locked the front door, hopped in my car, and proceeded to the golf course. Music blaring, windows open to a beautiful morning, I pulled into the parking lot to behold my friend removing her clubs from her trunk. ##%t! I forgot my clubs!

Practically performing a wheelie in the parking lot, I dashed back home, fretting I'd be late for our designated tee time. Pulling into the alley behind my garage, my stomach clenched. Where were the clubs? They had disappeared. Maybe they are still in the garage? No. Behind my gate? No. Did someone steal them?! Men from a lawn service were mowing the median behind my home. When I asked if they'd seen my clubs, one of them helpfully pointed to a townhouse two doors down. "A woman in a red car picked them up." I ran over and knocked, but no one answered. I kind of felt like I had fallen through Alice's rabbit hole. The experience just kept getting weirder. Meanwhile, our tee time was drawing near, so I headed back to the golf course to share clubs with my friends. Later in the day, I received a text from my neighbor. Thinking she was doing a good deed, Emmy had rescued my clubs, sticking them in her garage.

Dementia and/or Alzheimer's certainly are a fear as we age. I choose to believe that what people experience as a memory problem is often quite simply a not-paying-attention problem. I believe my experience that morning was a case of not paying attention or rather paying attention to too many things. I keep promising myself to be more mindful of the moment. Maybe this experience will be the impetus to really do so. That is, unless I forget.

Remember #7 in the *BBLB Manual of Maxims* says, "Cultivate a sense of humor"; laughing *with* yourself about these moments will certainly make them more tolerable. And besides, they make good stories.

THE ART OF A WASTED DAY

What is the opposite of mindfulness? To-do lists. That attempt we make to keep all those balls we are juggling airborne. Lady Boomers are especially attached to our to-do lists.

Remember the *Be Brave. Lose the Beige!* motto:

> Running from appointment to appointment, checking off the to-do list—that's not really living. Discovering the playful side of life. Spreading joy. Skirting a few rules. Being colorful... clever... creative. Now *that's* living!

I met a kindred spirit in Patricia Hampl, the author of *The Art of a Wasted Day*. She argues that since baby boomers are on the other side of striving, the to-do list is no longer as necessary.[3] Most of us relate to this notion of striving. Whether it is our careers, our children, or the pursuit of happiness, baby boomers strive and drive. Try yoga or meditation we are urged as a remedy for elevated blood pressure and insomnia from all the striving. But meditating is just one more thing. Yoga? Just another task to include on the to-do list.

Instead Hampl recommends, "How about just giving up? What about wasting time? Giving up or perhaps giving over. To what? Perhaps what an earlier age called *the life of the mind*, the phrase that describes the sovereign self at ease, the sheer value of looking out the window, letting the world float along."

I realize this is counter to the exercise prescription I just spent several paragraphs extolling. Mindfulness, however, is another worthy prescription in the BBLB arsenal.

Until Covid, I didn't know if I could execute this advice. I'm the ultimate multitasker. Give up?! Waste the day?! I've always maintained, maybe even with more than a little self-righteousness, that wasting a day is the ultimate sin. But like many other productivity-a-holics sheltering in place during the pandemic, we welcomed the reconciliation of time and space. Yes, we used some of that time to binge-watch favorite shows on Netflix and Amazon Prime Video, but we also were provided an opportunity to "spend aimless hours observing a spear of summer grass." Our souls got the chance to sneak up and whisper in our ears—kind of like God's whispers, where once we were too busy to hear.

Just before the onset of Covid, a beautiful city garden near my home featured an exhibit of large LEGO sculptures. I wandered in wonderment at the amazingly colorful, intricate structures. There were twelve of them, everything from a giant hummingbird to a peacock and birdbath, all constructed out of LEGOS. I'm proud to say that I did not get to every single one, as I was taking time to focus on the ones I saw. And I could literally feel the weight of my schedule release its grip as items from my ever present to do-list began to evaporate.

BBLB Manual of Maxims #19:
"Try wasting a day."

This therapy will calm your brain and promote mindfulness. "What's wrong? Why are you just sitting there staring out the window?" your partner might ask. "You should be doing this or that instead of just sitting on your butt," your inner voice might berate. Appropriate responses to these judgments? To your partner, I could suggest, "It's none of your business." To your inner critic, "I'm giving myself a break."

SEX OVER SIXTY

No BBLB Rx can be complete without a prescription for sex. Sex is no more of an on-limits topic after sixty than it was before sixty. Puritans founded the United States, and our attitudes toward sex have remained decidedly more puritanical than those of our foreign-born brothers and sisters. Even men who bragged with bravado about their sexual exploits during their younger years are now silent on the topic as they age into their third trimester. I would guess they have fewer such exploits to brag about, and they don't seem to be in a hurry to discuss their underperforming penises with friends. Even their partners appear reluctant to share details about their own post-menopausal issues or give up their husbands' sexual secrets. The subject is hard to talk about, and no, I'm not referring to the male organ.

While physical constraints can certainly serve as obstacles to intimacy, so do ego obstacles. I don't think I'm overstating it when I say an American man's definition of manliness is tied to his penis's performance. Pfizer has grossed tens of billions of dollars since 1998 when they launched their little blue pill for erectile dysfunction. Curious, I consulted two family psychologists with this question: Can a man be persuaded to believe that a fully functioning phallus is not required for intimacy? Studies document that women rarely define their sexual satisfaction or loss of desire based on the functioning of their sexual organs, but on the quality of their relationships. (Apparently the jury is still out for men.)

An erroneous belief is that sexual interest wanes with age; on the contrary, sexual desire runs deep among people in their fifties, sixties, seventies, and beyond, according to a 2021 article in *HealthDay*.[4] Sexual activity can also serve as a buffer against ill health and even contribute to cognitive flexibility.

But aging sex is not without its hardships. Even though there is no danger of pregnancy (at least for women), our sense of sexual freedom can still be punished by unprotected sex. I live a couple of counties away from a 125,000-member retirement community rumored to be a bed of promiscuity and STDs.

Okay, so let's bite the bullet and actually talk about sex over sixty. First, it's not generally very pretty. I think nature anticipated this problem, thus rendering the older set farsighted so up close and personal we can't really see all the lines, wrinkles, and bulges. Marital/partner longevity has its advantages at this stage of our lives, as our partners are accustomed to the state of our bodies. I dread having to break in someone new if something were to happen to my husband.

Second, forget about spontaneity or late-night spur-of-the-moment sex. We can't stay up that late, and there are certain forms of prescription preparedness often required. Just like when there were children in the house, it takes a measure of planning and commitment for sex to happen. An exchange between partners can sound something like this:

"Wait, I'll be right back. I need to take out my hearing aids."

"Oops! Not that side, my leg is still tender from arthroscopic surgery."

"Honey, can we switch sides? My wrist still hurts."

With so many painful parts, it would be easy to give up, but the physical and psychological benefits make the effort worthwhile. Intimacy is an essential component of being human, and our need for closeness certainly doesn't vanish on our sixtieth birthday. (A favorite *New Yorker* cartoon of mine features the grim reaper lurking over a young woman saying, "Happy 40ᵗʰ birthday! I'll be taking away the muscle tone from your upper arms, your amazing tolerance for caffeine, and your ability to digest French fries. The rest can stay.") Yes, our recurring birthdays have caused some erosion, but not the erosion of our need for contact and connection.

At our age, we don't have to choose between being naughty or nice. We can be as nice and grandmotherly as we choose but try sprinkling in a little naughtiness.

BBLB Manual of Maxims #20:
"Don't neglect romance." Touch is as important in our BBLB years as it ever was.

BBLB RECAP

The BBLB Rx pad prescribes these therapies for your aging journey:

Hold your dear friends dear. Breaking up with formerly functioning body parts can pitch you into a dark place. Friends come in handy supplying meals, comfort, and perspective.

Find the silver linings. Aside from friends, your attitude is your best companion in your BBLB years. Your attitude and the way you approach illness and injury will affect the quality of your days.

And for heaven's sake, don't beige up your life strategies. Choose to infuse even the most boring and mundane activities—like dieting and exercising—with color and fun. Good nutrition is even more important at this juncture. Eating in color is healthy and can be fun and imaginative. Redefine your version of athleticism; take baby steps toward physical fitness. Music is great for powering through a workout. The right playlist can improve the quality of your workout and your attitude.

Mindfulness is a must, and to-do lists are an anathema to mindfulness. Those incessant lists insist on pulling your attention forward rather than keeping it focused in the present. And I hesitate to mention the elephant in the room, but what if there isn't a tomorrow? Then we wasted all our focus on something that never came to be. Even "senior moments" can be a mindfulness issue. Those moments are more likely to be "not paying attention" moments.

Your Rx should include time for romance and/or touch. Covid taught us a lot about skin hunger. If at all possible, find snuggling opportunities. Intimacy offers a buffer against ill health and promotes mental health.

The potency (intensity) and dosage (frequency) of these prescriptions is up to you. But Beware: these therapies can be addictive.

EXERCISE YOUR CREATIVITY #4:

WASTE A DAY

Lady Boomers wear a lot of hats. We are simultaneously professionals, mothers, daughters, grandmothers, wives, volunteers, and board members. Multi-tasking all these roles can lead to "multi-taxing" our spirits.

BBLB's Rx for quieting our chatter-brains and addressing all this multi-tasking is to waste a day. For me, that often means a trip to the beach. Choose whatever destination affords you a place for meditation and contemplation.

Imagine yourself at the beach. Feel and smell the humid, salty air as you allow the ocean breeze to penetrate the schedules, to-do lists, and deadlines that live inside your overworked brain. During your time in the sun, envision yourself:

- reading a novel (nonfiction not allowed)
- frolicking in the water, delighting as you dive into the foamy washing machine waves, just like you did when you were a kid
- scouting for seashells and sand dollars
- walking along the water's edge at low tide

Now, why don't you go from imagining this scene to living it? It doesn't have to be the beach. You can find a park or give yourself a spa day. Just let it be someplace ➤

> away from home, to get you out of your familiar and responsibility-ridden environment. What would your ideal day off look like? Try journaling the thoughts bubbling up in your brain from all this spaciousness. What do you hear yourself saying?

CHAPTER 5:

Gummies, Pets, and Ex-husbands

"Pets understand humans better than humans do. They are human whisperers.""
—RUCHI PRABHU

Conspicuously absent from the Rx for Aging chapter was actual drug prescriptions. Since I do not hold any kind of medical license, I felt it prudent not to push pills. Gummies, however, are a drug of a different color. More than a closeted few sixty-plus-year-olds have been turning to marijuana to treat ailments associated with aging.

Another missing prescription? Pets. Pets bring the color! They introduce such playfulness into our lives. After years of struggling with obligations, the buoyancy these furry friends provide is balm for our tired spirits. They can also fill the intimacy gap. Nothing says intimacy like shoving your hand down the mouth of your golden retriever to retrieve the ball he's threatening to swallow.

And the third postponed prescription? Dump the dude! If you haven't done so already, consider how much freer you might feel unencumbered by a controlling partner. Hopefully I'm not describing your current plight, but if so, this segment is for you. This prescription is not offered cavalierly. It will require every ounce of bravery in your body. It certainly did for me when I dumped my dude at age forty. "Dude," by the way, euphemistically references any life partner, straight, gay, man, or woman.

Anxieties, arthritis, and financial fears often accompany us into our BBLB years. And they threaten to deplete us of our color and sass. I have not found aging resources and coping techniques that truly address the needs of the baby boomer generation. The techniques outlined in this chapter are guaranteed to introduce color, sass, and a lightness of spirit into your BBLB years. They will, however, require you to be brave and open-minded.

GOT GUMMIES?

Talk about a lightness of spirit! A 2016 article in *The Washington Post* noted that marijuana use among those fifty and older has ballooned since 2006.[1] (Waistlines have likely ballooned as well, given that marijuana promotes the munchies.) The article referenced a study that found Medicare reimbursements for a number of common prescription medications dropped sharply after the introduction of medical marijuana laws in many states.

Now perhaps marijuana use is not the healthiest coping technique, but this is a no-judgment zone. I'm just here to share the facts. I collect stories and this is a topic of interest to me since I, on occasion, have enjoyed the general sense of wellbeing and joint relief accompanying those Ganja-infused gelatin gems.

OUR FRIENDS JILL AND TODD recounted their herbal experience during a date night at a movie theater. As they are also in their BBLB years, I laughed and appreciated the precautions they took, which were a far cry from our youthful indiscretions.

Jill and Todd are in a second marriage. (They went through the equivalent of boot camp and a stint in the military in their first marriages and now in their second marital go round are enjoying their virtual medals of honor for bravery and service.) Therapy sessions had persuaded them they needed to interject more fun and playfulness into their lives. Both felt they had missed out on many of those formative, even somewhat reckless, experiences that tend to define the post-adolescent quest for independence. Jill's finances dictated that she had to put herself through college by working a lot, and an unexpected pregnancy made Todd a young father with multiple responsibilities.

Both of them dabbled in weed during the 1990s. Dopers, they weren't. A quarter of an ounce of marijuana would last them a year. But even without being high, they were often paranoid their teens would discover their stash. They'd hidden it in bags within bags, within purses on the top shelf in a closet. They told no one about their dirty little secret, and perhaps it was the secret that made it all the more fun. For short periods, two tokes on a joint helped them escape their multitasking and over-responsible selves. They laughed; they ate; they had sex; they watched movies. They felt young again. Which brings me to the updated point in their story when they no longer can be considered youngish.

A particular Thursday night brought the end of a rough week for Jill and Todd. Jill had unexpectedly been called to Atlanta in a childcare rescue effort after her daughter's babysitter quit. Three days of diaper changes, snotty noses, laundry, meal preparation, and airline travel had left her depleted. Todd, meanwhile, had been beset by annoyingly demanding clients while holding down the home front.

"I want to go to a movie!" Jill interrupted as he recounted how much he'd done during her absence. While Jill and Todd enjoyed movies, the stress of actually going out to a movie and having to be there at a precise time was not their idea of relaxing.

"Let's get high first," Jill suggested. They had recently received a box of cannabis-infused Colorado chocolates as a gift from friends.

"Ok, but I think we should take an Uber," her husband wisely suggested. Date night found them at the Regal Theater with a purse full of smuggled Five Guys burgers and glasses of wine from the movie bar. While their movie selection was a comedy, the howling and hysterics emanating from row F might have been a bit out of proportion to the actual humor quotient of the movie.

"Let's go to the Cheesecake Factory for dessert!" Jill cajoled her husband at the movie's conclusion. Jill and Todd were proud of the fact they were still up, dressed, and sitting at the restaurant bar at 10:30 at night on a work night (school night, as they liked to call it). Todd recounted how he had to take out his iPhone flashlight in order to be able to read the menu. And as the waiter was forced to repeat himself several times, Jill leaned over and all but shouted in an exasperated tone, "Did you forget to wear your hearing aids again?!"

I couldn't stop laughing listening to this story about

a boomer's version of getting stoned. Baby boomers are a responsible lot. Even as we contemplate retirement or semi-retirement, we can't seem to resist adding more to our plates. So maybe we can cut ourselves some slack when we engage in periodic distractions, like popping an edible every now and again (even if these indulgences are accompanied by hearing aids, iPhone flashlights, and ride share services). And talk about skirting the rules! "You're too old to be smoking weed," we imagine being told.

"Well, you don't know my bad ass generation then," should be your righteous response, after which you'll feel as light as air. And at our age, that's saying something.

THE DOCTOR SAYS IT'S OK!

A friend shared yet another weed story with me. I guess as we age, we become braver about disclosing our illicit habits (or maybe we're beyond caring).

Olivia enjoys a close relationship with her cardiologist. Even though she is fit and slender, she suffers from high blood pressure. As is the case for many people in their seventies, she is plagued with aches and pains which have not been assuaged by prescribed or OTC medications. A chance encounter with a sour-apple marijuana gummy, however, helped mitigate some of her complaints.

Reaching for the doorknob on her way out of a cardiologist visit, she casually said, "I'd like to talk with you about something I don't want you writing down on my chart."

"It must be weed," was the doctor's immediate response. "You probably want to ask me about the interaction between weed and your other prescriptions." She was floored.

"That is the number one question I get from women sixty and older," he continued nonchalantly. "The number one question from men of the same age is about Viagra. And no, you have nothing to worry about."

Who knew there was this underbelly of illicit drug use among baby boomers? Double confirming her cardiologist's opinion, Olivia checked with her primary care doctor, who supported the cardiologist's contention. "At least it doesn't hurt your liver like alcohol," the doctor said. "But I would urge you to grow your own. Then you know where it comes from rather than buying some from a mysterious source."

OMG! Grow your own weed?! Urged by doctors who have more credibility than most other professionals?!

BBLB Manual of Maxims #21:
"Got gummies?"

A TALE OF TWO DOGS

Pets are a metaphor for the plight of Lady Boomers. The coats of cats and dogs are generally some version of beige (cream, gray, brown). The survival of their ancestors depended upon these camouflage colors. Likewise, as we boomers survived parenting duties, career responsibilities, and aging issues, our coats too became beige.

Despite their limited exterior coloring, however, pets bring the color. They introduce such playfulness into our lives. After years of struggling with obligations, the buoyancy these furry friends provide is balm for our tired spirits. Pets are a great prescription for what ails us.

Baby boomers were the first generation to go all in

on pet ownership. Prior to this generation, dogs and cats were found more often in rural America, where they had jobs and subsisted off table scraps and outdoor scrounging. Baby boomers brought them inside and made them part of the family. Between 2008 and 2018, Boomer pet ownership grew to 54 percent. Baby boomers and their older counterparts account for 47 percent of pet expenditures. Apparently, once our nests emptied of humans, our maternal urges transferred to pampering our pets. And to some extent we have made them human substitutes. My husband and I anthropomorphize our dogs, inventing emotional scenarios that more than likely have no basis in fact. But it's fun and companionable. It makes us feel we're connected to a bigger family right inside our own house.

It has been said that the practice of ruling dynasties marrying into other reigning families has created physical and cognitive issues for the offspring of these intermarriages. This inbreeding has resulted in more than one descendant being labeled mad. The same can be suggested for purebred dogs. Those limited lines with their incestuous DNA have produced some cuckoo-for-cocoa puffs canines. And just in case I wasn't certain of this fact, I decided to buy not one but *two* pedigreed pooches.

We started with just the one Bichon Frise, weighing in at thirteen pounds. Manageable, right? That is, until the Madness of Queen Chloe began biting people. I'm not talking about a little nip at the heel; I'm talking about ankle biting sharp enough to draw blood. She bit our friends, she bit our family, she bit a trial lawyer! And he was really upset! But we didn't have the heart to put her down. She was a rescue dog purchase who came with "issues," or as my friend Suzan suggested, she was a repo dog, returned by the previous owners, no reason given.

Our self-esteem could not handle having such an inhospitable dog. (My husband and I fancy ourselves to be hospitable people, wanting our guests to feel warm and welcome, not screaming and bleeding). So, we did the only logical thing under the circumstances; we bought a second dog, a labradoodle puppy.

After spending the first weekend removing shoes, computer cords, and newspapers from needle-sharp teeth and talking nonstop about puppy pooping, I was hopelessly in love with our Jozy. So for the last several years we have enjoyed the company of a sixty-pound, sweet, charcoal grey, not too bright Labradoodle and a fifteen-pound mean, white, wicked-smart Bichon Frise. Chloe's the brains and Jozy's the brawn within this dynamic duo.

Chloe is a highly anxious soul, or as my southern grandmother used to say about people with similar temperaments, "She has a case of the nerves." As mentioned previously, her manner of coping with anxiety is to attack first, ask questions later. Chloe's skittish behavior has mandated that all family activities be performed en masse. (Her nerves are calmer when the family is together.) If Mom takes the recycling out, all four of us should take the recycling out. A trip to use the facilities should be done as a foursome. And, of course, cooking and eating is a joint family endeavor. The same applies to walks around our neighborhood. On a solo walk, Chloe's tail is in the down position, her already short legs sinking even lower. However, with Mom, Dad, and stepsister at her side, Chloe is all strut and attitude. "Ha!" we pretend Chloe says. "She's with me," (gesturing at Jozy) defying any person or pooch to take us on.

Jozy is oblivious to Chloe. She doesn't really care whether she sticks around or not. In fact, should the little one be receiving undue attention, or God forbid, affection, her large schnozz will find a way to intervene.

Thursday evenings around 6 p.m. are designated as "Dog's Night Out" at Enders Park near our townhouse. Dogs of all breeds and sizes run, fetch, and chase as their owners enjoy after-work libations. Chloe would have to take Xanax to cope with such an adventure. But Jozy, ever the extrovert, jogs up to people and pups alike as if to say, "Hello, how's it going?" No matter how often parents say things like. "I just want my children to be happy with who they are," deep down they yearn for acceptance, for their child to "fit in" and play well in the sandbox. That's my Jozy. She is well-adjusted. I watch her interactions with some measure of pride. Chloe's not the only one saying, "She (Jozy) is with me!"

PET EXPENSES ARE AS PRICEY AS KID EXPENSES ... AND WORTH IT

I don't remember when I started spending more money on my dogs than on my children, but our two high-class mutts take up a good bit of psychic, physical, and financial real estate in our home and budget. They must be walked twice a day (keeping the dog poop from overwhelming our 2000-square-foot back yard.) Their organic, grain-free, non-allergenic, senior dog food costs $70 a bag, two times per month. And don't get me started about the price of our vet bills (times two and the tech never fails to up-charge at every visit). And the barking! Oh, dear Lord. I'm always on edge about HOA complaints, or worse, eviction. Then there is the $50 per day charge for a dog sitter to stay in our house (because we can't risk boarding a biting Chloe) when we have the audacity to leave them for work or fun.

Our dogs are hyperaware of nuances—opening a certain dresser drawer cues them I'm about to put on a bra, which inevitably means I'm leaving the house. And Chloe takes her job as Chief of Security quite seriously. As deputy, Jozy's job is to use her deep, husky voice to scare away possible intruders. A squirrel passing gas three streets away elicits a good fifteen minutes of barking. Those two remind me of canine secret service agents. I often picture them in sunglasses alerting each other of our movements by talking into the wires concealed in their fur.

God forbid my husband and I make a move to go upstairs. That's when the murmuring commences: "They're heading up," Chloe whispers into her paw.

"Got 'em," comes the reply. "You coming? Why are they coming up here in the daytime? It's not bedtime. I don't get it. Wait, they closed the door, LEAVING US OUT," Jozy wails.

Chloe rolls her eyes. "For heaven's sakes, Jozy, it's been ten years. You know the drill by now. You know they can't live without us at their side. Mom and Dad just think they need a little alone time. Watch and learn, again," at which point she begins scratching and throwing herself against the door. "They will relent, feel bad about us, and let us in sooner than later," she says patiently, if not even a little patronizingly. Of course, she is correct, and within minutes, the door opens. Chloe, casting a self-satisfied glance back at Jozy, swaggers into the bedroom, assuming her rightful place. "Sure, they get a little mad, but it is easier to ask for forgiveness than permission."

Don't get me started about the grooming of these non-shedding, hypoallergenic breeds. They have hair in lieu of fur. The upside is they don't shed and leave vestiges of their coat all over the living room sofa. The downside is they must be groomed—and grooming is not cheap. About six times a year, we take our two for what we lovingly label a spa day. These spa days typically cost upwards of $170 once the tip has been included. Following one such visit, I asked Chloe if she enjoyed her experience. "What the hell do you think?!" she demanded. "They put their fingers up my butt, water boarded me like I was a terrorist at Guantanamo, and for intellectual torture threw me in a cell with a damned corgi, who, let's say it together, is an idiot. Then they stuck me into one of those damn tutus and put a bow in my hair like I'm some kind of useless frou frou dog!"

Jozy, rarely the complainer, always comes out looking as sleek and beautiful as a runway model. But this still goes down as a "no good deed goes unpunished" venture.

As much as I complain about my high-maintenance mongrels, they do bring color and spunk to my life. We project human characteristics onto these kooky kids, which makes us laugh.

REMEMBER, *BBLB MANUAL OF MAXIMS #7*: "Cultivate a sense of humor. It will keep you sane."

There is so much about the aging process that makes us feel insane. Anything we can do to introduce sanity back is worth the expense and trouble.

Pets made great companions during the throes of the pandemic. I experienced separation anxiety when we felt brave enough to take our first trip away from home (as I'm sure they did, too). Caring for others, even those with fur and feathers, keeps one from slipping into self-absorption and takes our minds off the anxiety of a scary medical diagnosis. Pets foster an environment of loving, a quality much in demand in our human world. (And best of all, they don't ask for a car or a college education!)

My hair stylist told me her labradoodle ate a one-hundred-dollar bill. She spent the next couple of days following her dog around collecting poop, on the lookout for paper in the stool. Her bank teller was less than thrilled when she presented her taped-together Benjamin Franklin. Pet ownership is an equation. On one hand, you have the expense and effort; on the other, the much-needed intimacy, love, and laughter.

BBLB Manual of Maxims #22:
"Try some pet therapy."

It's a lot of work, but you're unlikely to regret it.

DUMP THE DUDE

And the third postponed prescription? Dump the dude! Eating in color, taking a gummy, and adopting a pet are a breeze compared to this prescription. As I mentioned, I don't offer this cavalierly. It's complicated and will require every ounce of bravery in your body. It certainly did for me. (Disclaimer: I was forty, not sixty, when I dumped my dude. But the anxiety was comparable. I had two young children and felt massive financial insecurity.)

I've extolled the virtues of romance and sex, accompanied by recommendations for patience and adaptation. Intimate relationships are just as important as in previous decades, but not at the expense of our health and spirits. Abusive relationships take many forms. Physical is the most obvious. Emotional abuse is more insidious and often more subtle. Insults, humiliation, constant monitoring, and/or intimidation are demoralizing and erode the spirit. An acquaintance informed me that I was as beige as a wallflower while married to my first husband. (Unfortunately, she made this declaration in front of my daughter, who was not divorcing her father.) In retrospect, my divorce gave me the impetus for my *Be Brave. Lose the Beige!* blog. I got my color back following my divorce, and subsequently met the love of my life.

My first marriage gave me my precious children and grandchildren for which I'll always be grateful. It also enabled me to complete my college degree.

The courtship with my first husband consisted largely of his relentless pursuit. I took up smoking to avoid hand-holding. I wanted a friendship; Tim wanted love with a blonde, mini-skirt-wearing shiksa. His intelligence, wit, progressive politics, and Jewish identity intrigued me. We met working at the Legal Aid Society. He was working as a lawyer; I was working as a paralegal. My supervising attorney was afraid of poor people. Tim was not. I fell in love with him the night we sat in a pickup truck during a rainstorm in rural Central Florida. We were interviewing witnesses in a police brutality case. He cared. I liked that.

His pursuit wore down my resistance. I was introduced to fine dining, something my chronically empty wallet could not afford. Accepting his marriage proposal came with a guarantee of a honeymoon in New England. For a twenty-three-year-old girl who had never flown on an airplane, New England felt one thousand-plus miles out of my reach.

Our two week honeymoon was a fantasy. We ate clams on Cape Cod, attended a Boston Red Sox home game, and beheld paintings I'd seen only in textbooks at the Metropolitan Museum of Art. We had second row seats to two Broadway shows in New York. The Quebec Sovereignty Movement was in full force the summer of 1977, and coffee houses in Montreal reverberated with chants supporting French Quebecer's nationalism. The Quebecois people wanted to form their own nation within a united Canada. And we were right in the middle of it. It was exotic. I embraced these new experiences like someone stranded on a desert might react to discovering an oasis. My new husband was great on our trip. Attentive, fun, generous. Then we returned home to our non-fantasy lives.

I should have gotten a clue about his eccentric nature after we'd been selecting china patterns prior to our wedding. My mother, Tim, and I had lunch in the store's café. Observing two elderly women dining at an adjacent table, Tim asked, "Can I have those cream puffs if you aren't going to eat them?"

"No!" was the annoyed response.

There was also the time he tripped climbing over moviegoers en route to our theater seats as the lights dimmed for the movie previews. "Don't move!" he ordered, proceeding to scoop the popcorn from the lap of the horrified movie spectator. Friends and family members would roll their eyes at his antics. I did as well, but he made me laugh. Laughter and shared global values sustained us for twelve years.

Tim was globally sensitive and interpersonally dysfunctional. He went through two handkerchiefs slobbering and crying during a theater production of *Les Misérables*. The production is about courage, passion, and human resilience—global concepts his heart and mind could grasp.

I had young children, and I was not working when my mother died of breast cancer. I was thirty years old and her caregiver at the end of her life. My husband gave lip service to valuing my mothering and daughtering duties. His attitudes and actions indicated otherwise. He simply could not understand why so little was accomplished in our house during his absence at work. I had a nine-month-old, a terminally ill mother, and a pre-schooler; I felt lucky if I made it to the dry cleaner or folded a load of laundry prior to his arrival home.

Following my mom's death, I struggled with depression and feelings of worthlessness. I had no definition of myself other than caregiver. In his attempt at empathy, my husband said, "I can understand why you're feeling bad about yourself. I mean, look at all I've done during the past year. I'm a judge, I've written a book, I'm teaching at the University of Central Florida." He was genuinely perplexed when I threw a shoe at him. "I was empathizing with you!" he wailed. I'd never felt more alone.

Mother's Day coincided with this emotionally difficult time. The Saturday before Mother's Day, I followed a florist truck up my street. My heart skipped a hopeful beat. It turned into my driveway! I was thunderstruck, a big grin forming on my face. And then it backed out. My husband didn't stand a chance at that point.

I was journaling one night shortly before our separation and stumbled upon the realization that I had ceded most decision-making to my husband, which, I remember feeling guilty about. *Not only does he have to make judicial decisions all day*, I wrote, *he even decides what we're having for dinner at night.* Journaling has a sneaky way of revealing interior truths. "Wait, a minute." I said aloud to my pages. "His constant criticisms of my choices and suggestions have eroded my willingness to subject them to his scrutiny."

"He's not a bad guy," I would wail to our marriage counselor. "But I feel like he's the bull in the china shop, and I'm the china. My ego and emotions are broken and scattered all over the floor." It took all the bravery I had to separate. I was terrified I would end up without financial resources like my mother. But that didn't happen.

My friend Lydia accompanied me as my residency witness at my final divorce hearing. I was nervous. Walking up the courthouse steps, she slipped a joint in my purse. "This is a treat for after." I was so distracted I forgot there were x-ray machines and people searching purses and briefcases at the entrance to the building. Fortunately, the marijuana cigarette escaped notice.

All the anxiety and fear I experienced anticipating this D-day evaporated during my two-day beach escape that followed. I felt such a lightness of being. (The joint probably contributed to my lightened state.)

An avid tennis player, Tim picked up our son for a match one afternoon years after our divorce. "I joined a tennis league and just won my first match," I excitedly announced to my ex. "Who'd you play, somebody in a wheelchair?" he quipped. I probably laughed. I like to laugh. His wicked wit drew me in the first time. And this time I could laugh lightly and walk away. I was free from his control and judgment. I probably went back in my house to snuggle with my dog and take a gummy after the exchange.

BBLB RECAP

BBLB Manual of Maxims #23:
"Bravery is about saying yes, and . . ."

The world around you keeps telling you no. No, you shouldn't waste a day. You have too many things to check off on your to-do list to waste time. No, it's illegal and/or immoral to take a gummy. No, you've been with your partner for so many years, it's ridiculous to leave now. No, don't get a pet. They just pee on the rug and prevent you from traveling. No, no, and no.

All those no's put you in a box. It's time to exercise your sass. Poke fun at some of those societal no's. A less polite way of saying no is to say eff it. Between my arthritis and anxiety, I got a medical marijuana card and can buy gummies legally. Many states have passed medical and recreational marijuana laws, so you don't have to be reckless. Consult with your doctor. My sleep and moods have improved significantly. Loneliness, financial woes, and health problems are real issues. You need a reprieve. Pets offer intimacy, filling the gap left by absent partners and children. Those welcoming, wagging tails make us happy to come home.

And say yes to freedom. A controlling, abusive partner is not worth staying together just for the sake of staying married. A friend told me she was divorcing her husband after forty-five years of marriage. "Once I separated, I realized I would rather live in a cardboard box than stay in the house with him," she shared.

I'm not recommending refrigerator boxes as a home strategy. But put your creative thinking cap on and figure out a way to make yourself sassy again.

BBLB Manual of Maxims #24:
"If need be, dump the dude."

EXERCISE YOUR CREATIVITY #5:

SKETCH YOUR PET

Drawing challenges us to be brave. It's intimidating to make those first few lines. They tend to be wobbly and imprecise. Our inner perfectionist kicks in immediately and judges our efforts. "A five-year-old could have done a better job!" our inner critic admonishes. But those initial wobbles are the first step in a process. They are important. Refinement of those lines comes later.

Playing with drawing accomplishes three things: (1) It's one way we can exercise our creative muscles. Practicing creativity perpetuates creative thinking, which is helpful in our BBLB years. (2) It helps us be brave. Making those initial scribbles is scary—it's putting something of our true selves out into the world, and that makes us feel vulnerable. When we take the risk and rise to the challenge, however, we feel proud. (3) It's good for the brain. When we're drawing, we engage both sides of our brains, the right for creativity and the left for logical thinking. This strengthens both sides and helps us develop focus and strategic thinking. Drawing also releases endorphins, the happy hormone.

Spend twenty minutes sketching your pet. Take a photo and sketch from the picture if your furry or feathered friend refuses to sit still. A few tips:

It's best to use free flowing lines that are loosely and lightly drawn. To do that, adjust your grip on the ➤

➤ pencil so your hand is relaxed instead of tense. It's ok if your lines are wobbly or going in strange directions. Drawing is about layering.

When making an initial sketch, leave your perfectionism behind and focus on general shapes. The last thing you want to think about is detail.

A simple formula for drawing is (1) sketch loosely, (2) refine your sketch, (3) refine it again, and finally (4) define your sketch. In this last stage your lines will be more confident and tighter.

Happy Sketching.

CHAPTER 6:

The Power of the Purse

"Balls are to men what purses are to women."
—SARAH JESSICA PARKER

AH, THE PURSE. An inventory of a woman's closet often reveals an array of colors and sizes of purses. A shelf in my closet resembles a graveyard for the twenty-eight used and discarded bags. There are small bags, big bags, colorful bags. There are bags that are neutral, bags with too many pockets, and bags with too few pockets. I really liked them when I bought them at craft fairs and department stores, but I can't imagine why I still have them all. Some have lived on that shelf since I moved into our townhouse in 2015. A tag in a purse I purchased at an art festival says, "An interesting life is a choice." I probably bought the purse because of the inspirational tag. The tag lives in a small turquoise, chartreuse, and fuchsia bag shaped like a miniature tornado. It's a suitable metaphor for the interior of whatever purse I happen to be toting.

WOMEN HAVE A LOVE/HATE relationship with our purses. On one hand, they are absolutely essential for carrying those must-have items like cell phones, oversized wallets, keys, makeup, Advil, and pens. Purses have become mini mobile homes for our necessities. On the other hand, these purses require a seat all their own in restaurants and cars. No matter how many attempts I make at organizing my purse, it invariably ends up a toxic waste dump of used Kleenexes, crumpled masks, and uncapped lipstick smeared on the lining. But don't underestimate their significance. Our handbags are symbols of our power.

PURSES ARE LIKE VAGINAS

Many feminine accessories are used in subtle but powerful ways. Former Secretary of State Madeleine Albright delivered diplomatic messages without necessarily saying a word. She sent signals with her decorative pins and broaches. Former British Prime Minister Margaret Thatcher's handbag became her signature trope, as synonymous of her political career as Winston Churchill's cigar was for his. There was even a political cartoon of the former PM whacking Argentina with her purse. Likewise, Queen Elizabeth was rarely seen without her own color coordinated handbag. The Queen customarily wore her purse on her left arm. Switching it to the right arm signaled staff she wanted whatever conversation she was engaged in to be interrupted.

Purses are like vaginas. All the good stuff is hidden inside for only us to know about. That's our secret stash, and our partners know not to pillage our purses without permission.

Our ability to chuckle at our ambivalent relationship with our purses (and our vaginas) often belies the anxieties we feel about whether those bags hold sufficient resources to see us through our later years. And the statistics are scary. We are pretty sure our BBLB years will not resemble our parents' version of retirement. We may in fact be facing our "Golden Years" minus the gold. But perhaps we don't have to restrict our BBLB years to just one color. Let's put an innovative spin on baby boomer retirement options. Maybe even consider entrepreneurship. Self-employment makes sense because it allows for more control over working hours and conditions. And remember, as Lady Boomers, we love our control. And maybe we don't need as much gold as we thought we needed. The pandemic convinced me of that fact. Downsizing our spending does not mean downsizing our authentic quality of life.

Don't you have a fantasy in your head about what retirement might look like? Can your purse accommodate your retirement fantasies? If the answer is yes or probably yes, that is fantastic. The peace of mind that comes with financial security is irreplaceable. If the answer is "not quite," then we adapt. We have adapted and adjusted all our lives. Why would this segment be any different? So "stretch" may be a useful word in our BBLB years. Stretching our limbs helps us remain physically flexible. Stretching our expectations may introduce us to opportunities we hadn't considered before. We might need flexible expectations of our purses as well. This new attitude may empower your purse in a whole new way.

BBLB Manual of Maxims #25:
"Accepting the state of our purses equals accepting ourselves." (The same can be said of our vaginas.)

THIS IS NOT YOUR PARENTS' RETIREMENT

Research studies report our purses may be missing a few coins. A 2019 Transamerica Center for Retirement Study found:

> More than half of American Baby Boomers plan to work past 65 or not retire at all. The reason being—many people have limited savings; others are afraid they will outlive their savings; and still others fear incurring a long-term illness and extended medical expenses.[1]

How, pray tell, did we get here? Obviously, several financial crises contributed. Another factor is communication. Especially with girls. Growing up, I was cautioned to avoid talking about money, politics, and religion in polite circles. (Polite circles? Seriously?! What does that term even mean?)

Considering our fractured country and its political and religious divisions, that counsel was probably wise. But perhaps this social mandate shouldn't have applied to finances since many of us came up short in saving money for our retirements. Our retirement incomes simply haven't increased commensurate with the increase in our longevity. Life expectancy has increased by 50 percent in the last one hundred years.

A 2019 *CNBC* report found that women tend to leave crucial financial decisions to their husbands and partners.[2] I know I have ceded a lot of control of my finances to my current and former husbands. I'll even confess that I've had no input in preparing and filing my income taxes for over thirty years. I'm sure there are many women who are financially literate. The rest of us, however, require more education.

According to the Bureau of Labor, prior to Covid, one of the fastest-growing age groups in the employment sector were people over the age of sixty-five. And employers are embracing, even nurturing the trend by offering flex schedules and longer vacations. Boomers aren't necessarily eager to take jobs away from younger workers; they need the money. Forty-five percent of baby boomers have no savings and must rely on Social Security benefits for their income.

I don't aspire to the kind of retirement my parents enjoyed. My father retired at fifty-five, played golf three times each week, fit in a tennis match or two, participated in bridge tournaments, and traveled the country. I don't care about playing golf three times a week (although one would be nice). None of my friends play bridge, so that fantasy is out. I like to travel, but I think I'm just going to have to fit it in between work gigs. My priorities and fantasies have had to change to accommodate my pocketbook. What remains a priority for most of us though is achieving financial security, tending to our health, devoting time to a cause or passion we care about, and spending time with friends and family members. Even in my late sixties, I'm not planning to retire until my mental and physical health dictate I do so. For many of us, the 2008 recession wacked our purses.

THE GOLDEN YEARS MINUS THE GOLD

The Great Recession of 2008 depleted a lot of our gold. It took a heavy hit on pensions and 401(k) savings plans. Post 2008, "The Golden Years" is not exactly how I would characterize this phase of our lives.

Conducting research for this book, I interviewed Lady Boomers about the state of their purses. Many referenced the recession as the source of their financial anxieties. Carol (age seventy) said she was at 75 percent of where her savings had been in 2008 but anticipated working a couple of days each week as long as she was able. Barbara and Bob, both in their late sixties, planned to retire in 2020. The recession nixed that dream. Barbara returned to work as a nurse to help replenish their savings. Fred (age sixty-five), a former financial advisor, said his savings took such a hit he and his wife had to rent out a room in their home. Fred got a job at a local restaurant and literally took up singing for his supper.

My empathy went into hyper-drive hearing these tales. The recession knocked my 401(k) plans for a loop. Like the people cited above, my husband and I have steadily but not yet fully replenished our savings and have no intention of retiring until it is absolutely necessary. Just like so many small businesses across the country, we have had to pay 100 percent of our health insurance premiums and fully fund our own retirement accounts.

A 2021 article in the *Christian Science Monitor* noted that the pandemic had a profound impact on Boomer retirement.[3] The Covid crisis provided Americans golden opportunities to evaluate their work lives, transition to the golden years, and decide what they want their later lives to look like. The article went on to say, "By September 2020, more boomers had retired in the previous twelve months than in any year since the oldest boomer turned sixty-five."

So, between the Great Recession and the pandemic, our generation has been on a financial seesaw. Do we retire and live with less or continue working as long as we're able? Will our "Golden Years" be spent sans the gold? If that is in fact the case for many of us, creative thinking is even more vital in navigating what's next. America has done a poor job of getting its society ready to accommodate a lot of its people living a lot longer. In spite of our numbers, designers seem to have it out for the older among us. Food and drug containers require wrenches to open or the strength of Hercules to twist. Instructions for any purchase come with such small font a flashlight or magnifying glass is required. The same is true for restaurant menus. If the design engineers do deem to create products for the older set—raised toilet seat or shower chair—the product screams, "Hey, look at me, I'm old!"

I was reading the Sunday paper (yes, I still call my digital edition of the *Orlando Sentinel* "the paper") one fall morning in 2021. The Doonesbury cartoon demonstrated the difference between men and women in retirement. It featured two female retirees and their husbands. Like toddlers' parallel play, the husbands engaged in one conversation, the wives in another. The men traded banalities about their superficial activities.

"Did you hear about my big putt?"

"On the 17th? Yeah, amazing!"

"I'm almost as busy as I was on Wall Street," says the guest.

"Doing what, Ed?"

"Oh, you know, this, that, and the other thing," he shrugs. Frame by frame, the men gradually disappear as the women discuss the prison reform chapter in their masters thesis project. "You should bring your thesis to book club. We could start a GoFundMe page to support your work." Women will figure out finding meaning in retirement. Men? I question their adaptability.

SAY HELLO, NOT GOODBYE, TO YOUR GOLDEN YEARS

Again, with the golden years! Let's label them Magenta years. One way to empower our purses is to think entrepreneurially.

In November 2016, the Global Financial Literacy Excellence Center convened a panel of experts from the Small Business Administration, US Bureau of Labor, and AARP to discuss the idea of entrepreneurship among baby boomers.[4] They reported that self-employment among older people had become increasingly prevalent. Entrepreneurship offers flexibility and a gradual path toward retirement. Retirement havens across the country are boasting similar self-employment patterns, putting an innovative spin on the topic of baby boomer retirement.

SELF-EMPLOYMENT MAKES SENSE because it allows for more control over working hours and conditions. Speaking of control, if we pursue self-employment or dabble as entrepreneurs, let's try to control the work environment. Many of us have spent years waking up at 6:00 a.m. to get ready for a job we found depleting. But if we're not going to be able to kick back, drive a golf cart, and play bridge all day, let's envision a different kind of retirement for ourselves. Here are a few suggestions:

- You have spent years trying to fit exercise in to your work life, often arriving at the gym by 5:30 a.m. Reverse the scenario and make sure your employment endeavors accommodate your exercise schedule.

- Choose an enterprise that fits your circadian rhythm, one that allows you to both arise and go to bed at times best suited for you.
- Delve into your psyche through journaling or quiet reflection to explore what you have a passion for. You may want to undergo a personality assessment to discover a field that suits you (one is included at the end of this book).
- Make your entrepreneurial efforts flexible so technology can allow you to be anywhere and still work.

Here's to meeting your entrepreneurial self.

FAILURE'S JUST ANOTHER WORD FOR CREATIVITY

One obvious deterrent to engaging in entrepreneurial efforts is the fear of failure. That fear can be debilitating and certainly capable of halting plans we deem risky. That's one reason I blatantly eavesdropped on a conversation between a couple of thirty-something men one morning at my favorite independent coffee shop haunt. They were discussing the tech industry's attitude toward failure in Silicon Valley. "Failure means you just haven't gotten your success yet," one man said to the other. "Failure is mandatory; it's as pervasive as the weather. The fear of being a failure drives you," responded the other. They were so passionate I assumed they had recently listened to a TED Talk on the topic or had just stepped out of a motivational meeting on tech business startups. Their conversation, however, made me rethink the concept of failure. Generally, the word has negative associations, but their perspective was so positive.

My husband and I consider ourselves to be entrepreneurs, and we find the process of conception (much like that other kind of conception process) is the fun part—the brainstorming process, the excitement of a new idea, the hope of making the idea an income producing one. To be honest, many of our ideas have not produced a sustainable source of income. I've come up with some doozies that have to be considered failures since they cost me more money than I made. I wanted desperately to make money from my clay creations. I tried selling my polymer clay sculptures at art shows and farmer's markets, to no real avail. I designed "Jack" magnets featuring a boxing political donkey which I tried selling at Democratic conventions and events. I tried making two-dimensional images out of my three-dimensional sculptures. I sold posters, mugs, and greeting cards with images of my clay art pieces. And in each case, I failed to sell enough to recoup my financial investments. But all these "failures" put me on a trail that led me to endeavors that have been valuable and even successful. My love of clay led me to create The Jeremiah Project, an after-school and summer pottery program for under-served kids. Providing an opportunity for kids to explore their creativity and develop creative thinking skills "counts" as a success, and I earned a living directing the program to boot! Creating the text for my greeting cards and posters made me realize I love writing. I started my

Be Brave, Lose the Beige! blog in 2009, which led me to write this book. You just never know where the trail will lead once you are brave and take that leap of faith. In response to a question about his missteps, Thomas Edison once said, "I have not failed 10,000 times–I've successfully found 10,000 ways that will not work."

If you think you might consider an entrepreneurial endeavor, look first in your own backyard. How can you use your sixty plus years of living to inform your next venture? There is a myriad of concierge services you can invent, many of them focused on assisting others in their BBLB years:

- Consult with home design and safety issues for seniors who want to age in place in their own homes.
- If you're skilled at home repairs, remember that many others are not. Rent yourself out for odd jobs. (Just try to avoid ladders. They're death traps for people our age.)
- Become a clutter consultant. As we age and downsize, what do we do with all this stuff?! It's not fair to leave it for our children for future culling and sorting. You can be assured they don't want our stuff.
- Become a house and pet sitter. We have more flexibility now and have more availability (and more pets!)
- Much like travel agents of yore, use your vast travel experiences to help others plan their adventures and getaways.
- If you love shopping, become a personal shopper for clothes, food, and gifts.

- Use your financial or legal background to provide guidance for others.
- If you fancy yourself a chef, write a cookbook or start a meal delivery business.
- Become a nutritional or fitness consultant.

The world needs what you know. You are a treasure trove of experiences; why keep all that valuable knowledge just for yourself?

AGEISM CALLS FOR AN ATTITUDE ADJUSTMENT

It seems older people are biased against older people reports *New York Times* writer, Peggy Klaus in her 2013 "Embrace Your Age and Conquer the World":

> *I talked to a manager in her sixties who acknowledged that she was reluctant to hire a 64-year-old candidate out of concern that he/she wouldn't stay for more than a year or two before retiring.*[5]

But Klaus argued that many baby boomers want to keep working past the traditional retirement age. "They like the stimulation and the challenge. Many need to work. When there are mortgages, college tuition, and elderly parents to deal with, retirement is not an option."

I don't know about conquering the world so much, but maybe trying to conquer our own world is a worthy pursuit. Klaus argues that despite, or perhaps because of, ageism we baby boomers should "start to own, even embrace, how old we are." She says it's the perfect time for a major cultural attitude adjustment. Her book cites a Northwestern University study in which the author, Benjamin Jones, opined that people fifty-five and even sixty-five have more innovation potential than twenty-five-year-olds.[6]

I agree with Peggy Klaus and Benjamin Jones. This is a perfect time for a major cultural attitude adjustment, and let's start with us–the boomer generation. After all, there are a lot of us, almost 80 million. At this age, like any other, the key to happiness is to fully embrace who we are—to prize what we've learned and to appreciate how far we've come. Because many of us will be around into our late 80s and 90s—and maybe longer—we'll have lots of time to practice.

"STAY HUNGRY, STAY FOOLISH."

"Stay Hungry, Stay Foolish." I was reminded of these words from Steve Jobs' 2005 commencement speech at Stanford University as we watched a movie about the man. The movie simultaneously portrays Steve Jobs as a heartless opportunist and a creative visionary. Regardless of the characterization, Jobs was a fascinating guy who brought us the likes of MacBooks, iPads, iPhones, and AirPods. The movie depicted him as algorithm obsessed and relentless in his pursuit of the perfect product design. Geniuses are a little lopsided. And Steve Jobs was, apparently, pretty lopsided— brilliantly creative and interpersonally dysfunctional. Jobs was invited to give the commencement address at Stanford University in 2005, ironic since he admitted that he had never graduated from college. "Truth be told," he said, "This will be the closest I will ever get to a college graduation." He went on to advise:

*"Stay hungry . . . stay eager. Stay foolish . . . try new
things, step out of your comfort zone. Your time is limited, so don't waste it living someone else's life. Don't
be trapped by dogma—which is living with the results
of other people's thinking. Don't let the noise of others'
opinions drown out your own inner voice. And most
importantly, have the courage to follow your heart
and intuition. They somehow already know what you
truly want to become. Everything else is secondary."*[7]

I don't think this advice has a timestamp or an age limit.
As we age into these *BBLB* years, don't settle for living
someone else's life. I don't believe it is ever too late to pursue
our postponed dreams and follow our heart and intuition.
If you aren't willing to be foolish now, then when?

BBLB Manual of Maxims #26:
"Stay foolish."

THE POWER OF THE PURSE

The year I turned sixty, I facilitated a workshop at a women's
retreat. The intergenerational session was entitled, "The
Power of the Purse." Many of the participants in the session
belonged to the generation *Time Magazine*, in a 1951 cover
story, labeled, "The Silent Generation." Born between1925
and 1945, this was a generation that didn't issue manifestos,
participate in protests or demonstrations, or carry placards
and posters. One of the characteristics of people from this
group has been their silence. While the wonderful qualities
of this generation are numerous, a dominant characteristic
historically has been their reluctance to stand up to

"authority." And for many of the women in this group, that authority figure often took the form of their husbands.

The resounding refrain among these silent generation women was how little control they exercised over their household purse strings. Some of it was by choice, as was the case for a lady from Barbados. Following her move to the United States, she ceded many of the financial responsibilities to her husband. This posed a problem upon his death when she was left with little to no experience in balancing a checkbook or paying taxes. That choice did not belong to another workshop participant, who shared that her controlling husband allowed her no input into their family's financial matters. Since his death, she has found it liberating to take control of her own money. She buys gifts for herself (something her husband rarely did), saying, "Thank you for my sweet present, Jack."

Another woman, happily ensconced in a twenty-five-year second marriage, discussed the ego depletion of her first. Her first husband not only allowed her little to no monetary input but also didn't permit her to even have a driver's license.

My mother made major purchases (a new Hi-Fi and television, for example) while my father was away for his two-week stints each summer at his Army Reserve summer camp training. She decided it was easier to ask for forgiveness than permission from this man, for whom "no" was an automatic response. Subterfuge and manipulation gave some women of that generation a modicum of financial control.

I had little to no control over my own family's purse strings in my first marriage. I remember pleading with my husband to buy a color television. "Tracy doesn't even know Big Bird is yellow," I wailed one morning, referring to our two-year-old daughter. Taking matters into my own hands, I enlisted the help of Tim's best friend. George, aware of Tim's penchant for frugality, agreed to accompany us to Circuit City. Tim whined the entire way there about spending the money, but he was outvoted. I bought the TV. Whimpering, Tim curled up in a fetal position in George's back seat for the ride home. I realized the power of the purse that night, and within a couple of months, I got a job. Regardless, Tim's self-professed goal was to make more money writing his book (his side business) than I made in my part-time job. This power struggle depleted my color, and I was beige for many years. I finally dumped that dude.

It's never too late to empower our purses, and by extension, our lives. It may require bravery and a sprinkling of creative thinking, but it can be done. One brave friend, Kathy, really wanted to travel but was insecure about her income. She tried a gap year as a trial run at retirement.

A GAP YEAR FOR GROWNUPS (NO, UNLIKE TRIX CEREAL, GAP YEARS AREN'T JUST FOR KIDS)

Sixty-three-year-old Kathy was growing increasingly restless in her position as a relationship banker at Bank of America. She was tired of feigning interest in the lives of her wealthy clients and their overindulged adult children. She was also anxious about early mortality since no one in her mother's family had lived past the age of sixty-nine.

"I wanted desperately to travel. There was so much yet for me to see. I was divorced at forty-five, so if I didn't take myself, no one else would."

A casual comment from a colleague, whose son was heading out to take a gap year before college, sent her head spinning with possibilities. "Why can't I take a gap year in anticipation of my retirement?"

Sometimes the planning and anticipation of a trip is half the fun of the overall adventure. A six-month frenzy ensued as she submitted her sabbatical notice and planned her excursions. Kathy wasn't known for her adventurous spirit, so her friends were aghast at her haste. Kathy sold her house, put furnishings in storage, and basically said "Ta ta" to long time pals and relatives. "And she didn't even ask any of us to go along!" wailed a wannabe world-traveler acquaintance.

The grumblings were accompanied by grudging respect, however. It was a brave thing for her to do, especially considering her savings had taken a hit during the 2008 recession. But many of her excursions provided room and board; some even came with a modest stipend, like her two-week stay at an elephant sanctuary in Thailand. Living conditions were a far cry from her suburban Philadelphia digs, but there was running water, toilets that flushed, and three vegetarian meals a day.

Protecting the vulnerable defined Kathy's adventures. Her second tour took her to South Africa to a home for neglected and abused girls. Tending organic fields in Scotland and attending a writing retreat in North Carolina were also a part of Kathy's gap experiences. Her fiction-writing hobby blossomed into the publication of two collections of short stories subsequent to her sabbatical. "I never would have thought of making that kind of stretch before," she said after returning from her adventures.

And that is the key word: stretch, to introduce yourself to opportunities and avenues you never knew you might enjoy. We have spent so much of our lives in service to an employer, our children, our parents, friends, and even volunteer boards, that in many cases we've left very little time to explore creative ventures that might be self-fulfilling.

A 2017 *NEW YORK TIMES* ARTICLE entitled, "You Don't Have to be College Bound to Take a Gap Year," featured seventy-four-year-old oncologist John Siebel who wanted to retire but treat patients part time. Dr. Siebel's version of a gap experience involved becoming a temp covering for vacationing oncologists in locations where he wanted to travel. He booked short stints in remote parts of Alaska, California, and Idaho near wilderness areas. Weekdays found him seeing patients, weekends exploring mountains and wilderness areas. "Dr. Siebel blurred the lines between work and leisure, re-defining the traditional ideas about the nature of retirement."[8]

A growing number of older Americans are experimenting with the concept of a self-designed retirement. Even if we don't have Dr. Siebel's skill set, we have our own set of important skills, which can often enable us to have work flexibility.

So, whatever you want to call it—gap year, semi-retirement, work flexibility, or a self-designed retirement, this is not your mom's and dad's version of retirement. We have deferred, deflected, and denied our interior selves for too long. Let's be the boss of ourselves in this next phase.

OK, BOOMER

I have spent time in this chapter bemoaning the financial crises that have pitched boomer retirement options into uncertainty. Well, younger generations apparently don't see our woes in the same light. My millennial son sent me a link to a song that premiered in March 2021 on *Saturday Night Live* entitled "Boomers Got the Vax." The song satirizes baby boomers as the greatest generation and the first age group to get the Covid vaccine. "Got all the money, now we got the vaccination. Crash the economy, three whole times, but when it comes to the vax, we the first in line." Apparently there is more resentment among millennials toward their baby boomer parents than I'd realized.

"OK boomer" is a phrase and internet meme mocking baby boomers. According to a 2020 article in the *New York Times*, "OK boomer" marks the end of friendly generational relations.[9] Bottled up frustration and annoyance at the attitudes and policies of the baby boomer generation apparently drives this meme. Responsibility for worsening climate change, economic hardship, and political polarization is being placed squarely in the laps of boomers.

I admit to feeling stunned by this assessment. *They're talking about us*?! I ruminated. *I thought they liked us. I thought we were the cool ones.* I spent an entire chapter in this book enumerating the ways boomer moms have sacrificed, supported, even enabled our kids at the expense of our pensions and passions. But apparently, the economic prospects of millennials and Gen Zers have been sacrificed to help greedy, ungrateful boomers.

Their assessment is humbling and maybe a little accurate. Even if it's out of economic necessity, we're the ones hanging around in jobs which could be filled by members of younger generations. Student loan debt is at 1.7 trillion, our environmental policies have wreaked havoc with our planet, and we may be the last generation to fully enjoy Social Security and Medicare benefits. Projections are bleak. The Social Security Fund is expected to be exhausted by 2034.

I guess that is the natural order of things: younger generations resent and disparage older ones. And we *have* been a little full of ourselves. We have kind of behaved like the evil queen in *Snow White and the Seven Dwarfs*, "Magic mirror in my hand. Who's the fairest generation in the land?" The magic mirror and all the industries catering to us throughout our lives have always responded, "You are the greatest." I guess we should stop whining.

SENIOR COMMUNES

People who have a good bit of gold are moving into expensive senior living facilities. These facilities include meals, housekeeping, health care, exercise facilities, art centers, and educational opportunities. A facility near my home describes itself as "A Personal Oasis." I doubt if I'm alone in envying the fortunate few who can afford to live in places like this. But what if your purses lack the gold to afford such a lifestyle? Yes, I feel certain our kids will step up and help, but do we want them to have to? I don't want to impose on their lives or have them witness my physical failings. I also don't want them bossing me around. My son already removes sharp knives from my hands when I'm preparing meals for his family, fearing I might injure myself. ("Do you know how many carrots I've cut in my lifetime!" I retort.) I like my independence, and I imagine you do as well. So if we aren't Queen Midas, I think we're going to have to don our creative thinking hats and develop new strategies for making our BBLB years golden.

Remember communes? In the 1960s and 1970s, hippies and dreamers set out to build a new communal culture separate from established society. The operative word was "share." Shared living spaces, shared daily living tasks, shared parenting responsibilities, and shared resources. It was a pretty inventive idea, one that defied the standards of establishment living. I lived in a commune for a year when I was nineteen. Living with six others in a three-bedroom, two bath cinder block house, however, was not my vision of utopia. But maybe it's a concept worth considering in our BBLB years. Women are very good at creating communities. We've done it all our lives. So, what if we once again step outside the lines and choose an updated communal model for living in our BBLB years? We learned what we didn't like about communal living in the past—mainly the lack of privacy; so maybe now we can get it right. Private living space is a must. I don't want to share a room with someone other than my husband (and that's even iffy on occasion). Maybe our second operative word after "share" is proximity. We could live in proximity to our favorite friends. And I'm not necessarily referring to plus-fifty-five-year-old residential communities. I don't want to be separate from younger and older people. I enjoy hearing children laugh and ride their bikes down my street. An objective of this effort could be developing authentic communities in real neighborhoods. Not ones separated by geography and age.

We would rely upon each other for managing everyday tasks. Grocery shopping, meal preparation, and transportation could be shared responsibilities. Each person would assume tasks appropriate for their strengths and physical abilities. I know it would take some negotiation to achieve agreement between all of us independent, opinionated boomers. But it could work, and the consequences of it not working might be costly for our purses and independence. Proximity even helps with shared cleaning services and home health care personnel. We are already witnessing the emergence of a sharing economy, so this transition may not be such a dramatic one. I think the sense of community will add color and richness to our lives.

BBLB Manual of Maxims #27:
"Live in community with one another."

Our neighbors are more important than ever.

BBLB RECAP

We have concluded that our retirement purses are not likely to resemble our parents' purses. We may be facing our Magenta (I'm done with Golden) Years sans the gold. We might have to continue working to extend our retirement income. But we are living longer and more actively, so this is to be expected. What we do have control over is our attitude. We're going to boldly resurrect our 1960s attitudes and rebel against establishment aging standards. If this is our fate, let's try to control our fortune.

Take your retirement a little at a time. Maybe you have already done this throughout your work life.

If not, start now. Take a sabbatical, do a gap year. Find a way to get it partially subsidized.

Try self-employment. Entrepreneurship is *in* among our generation. Develop the business you have always wanted to have, doing something you love.

Abbreviate your work hours. Two days instead of five; noon to five instead of early morning. A little extra income goes a long way in stretching your purse.

Consider a communal living arrangement. Communal living cuts expenses and helps us maintain our dignity, pocketbook, and independence.

Facing these issues, planning for them, and imagining the possibilities is brave. Demonstrating this kind of bravery will add vigor and sass back into your life and your purse.

EXERCISE YOUR CREATIVITY #6

EVALUATE YOUR PURSE

Evaluate your go-to purse. What does it look like? What about the texture, size, and color drew you to this purse? Does it say you're organized, whimsical, practical, outdoorsy? What's inside? Are there lots of pockets or hardly any? Are your sunglasses, cell phone, and keys assigned to particular pockets? How much money do you carry on your person? How many credit cards do you have? Do you have a credit card (or more) that's in only your name? What about your checking account? Is it a joint account or in your name only? Do you carry makeup? Is your appearance in the outside world important to you? What are the essential items in your bag? Which items could be removed?

There are no right or wrong answers in this exercise. It's just a fun sneak peek at what you value. What one thing can you change about your purse that might feel empowering?

Write your responses to these questions on a piece of paper. Answer the questions as quickly as possible to hear your instinctive voice. Once your initial answers are written down, go back through and refine them. Take a break for a day or so and then come back to your responses and read them again.

- What jumps out at you?
- What do you hear your purse saying about you?
- How do these answers describe you?
- How accurate do you think they are?

Give yourself permission to buy a new purse, and make sure there's at least one element of sass to the purchase.

BBLB Manual of Maxims #28:
"Your purse doesn't have to match your clothes."

CHAPTER 7:

The Reluctant Angel

"My guardian angel just filed a restraining order against me."
—DT KRIPPENE

I've been thinking about angels. I've observed a consistent few who are first in line to provide transportation, meals, and other heavenly concoctions to injured and ailing friends. I'm touched by the angels among us willing to share their purses with those in need. Beyond cosmic cherubs, I'm also referring to those real live people who step forward to take on emotional responsibility for others. These angels don't sprout wings or have halos. They aren't showy and don't need to be the focus of attention. More than likely, they've been drawn to one of the helping professions–therapist, minister, social worker, or health care professional. A defining angel attribute is their ability to listen–with undivided attention and seemingly without judgment. These angels often offer good advice for addressing anxiety-invoking issues, so it's easy for the beneficiaries of this attention to come down with angel addiction.

Even the self-sufficient among us, if given half an opportunity, will readily dive into the angel's amniotic fluid, languishing in their warm, nurturing, healing presence. Angels beware: supporting others and offering shoulders as crying platforms can lead to torn rotator cuffs and stress fractures. Just because angels appear to be adept at shouldering burdens does not mean they escape the emotional impact of these encounters. There is a pattern to these encounters: The recipient (1) pushes the panic button, (2) off loads their worries and anxieties on to the angel, (3) feels better, and (4) leaves the angel to clean up the emotional mess and to absorb the anxiety.

BEWARE: ANGELS CAN BECOME GLORIFIED TRASH CANS

"Trash can" may be a better description of the roles these angels serve.

I don't profess to be an angel, but as I near the end of my sixtieth decade, I've concluded I'm a trash can. I'm an ever present and obviously convenient receptacle for people's garbage. And because trash cans have lids, people think once they've deposited their gaseous garbage, the lid will seal, and their crap won't stink any longer. The same expectation applies to the angel. Once the dump is done, the angel's lips seal, preventing others from getting a whiff of the garbage. You can see the relief on the faces of the depositors; you can hear the lilt in their voices indicating how much better they feel. The angel, meanwhile, is left holding the bag of the dumper's treasure trove of trash. The panic and anxiety, once belonging to the dumper, now belongs to the angel. But perpetrators don't stop to think that angels must contend with their own ration of refuse. The added anxiety bloats and fills them beyond capacity.

Are you a reluctant angel? It can feel good to be needed. It feels like an honor to be privy to the intimate details of someone's life. Until it dawns on you that the honor has morphed into an imposition. It's at this point that sainthood flirts with martyrdom. Maybe, like municipalities, we need to institute a new waste management system. So many problems addressed by angels are recycled issues. Garbage recycling separates plastics, paper, glass, and metals; similarly, sorting and separating genuine problems from petty ones can keep your trashcan from becoming overwhelmed. Or how about this: friend, family member, hair stylist, random grocery store clerk—try using *your own* trash cans and recycling bins to deposit your rubbish.

So what happens when the trashcan overflows and anxiety leaks out all over your life? Anthropomorphizing it, giving it a name and personality can help you step back and gain perspective.

ANXIETY SPEAKS SOFTLY AND CARRIES A BIG STICK

Unwelcome visitors tend to pop in at the most inopportune and unexpected times. The telephone is one such an intruder, its shrill ring interrupting sacred downtime. Back when we were still tethered to landlines, sans caller ID and Sarah's was the voice on the other end of the line, I would sink into the adjacent chair dreading the next forty-five-minute interruption of whining and wailing.

I have a reoccurring unwelcome visitor who chooses to interrupt me at the most vulnerable times. Most frequently it's at first light, "cockcrow time" I've heard it called. She slips into my king-size bed and spoons with me, whispering softly into my barely awake ear. I watched this totally weird television show for a short while. It was called *Braindead*. In this satire, extraterrestrial insects invaded the brains of politicians, taking control of their lives and political views. Their point of entry was the ear. My early a.m. visitor does the same thing to me. Like smoke, she wafts into my ear, and I begin coughing and choking from the doubt and judgment she imparts.

My companion spells her name A-N-X-I-E-T-Y. Anxiety is non-gender specific, but I would feel a little unfaithful to my husband attributing male characteristics to my virtual visitor as she slips in bed with me in the wee hours of the morning.

I am accustomed to her periodic pop-ins, but my intruder's relentless presence during my spate of injuries and Covid propelled me into a dark place. It's disconcerting because, living in Florida, I live in the light. This darkness feels unfamiliar. I wonder if this is what it feels like to live near the Shetland Islands or a Nordic country close to the Arctic Circle. But I suspect what I was feeling was not geographically induced.

Anxiety is kind of like a mean mother-in-law or insecure professor who makes you feel you can't do anything right. "You know your SEP account is tanking, and you won't have money left to live on in retirement," she hisses into my barely awake ear. "Your husband was coughing last night. I'll bet he has the virus."

"You call yourself a writer?!" she snorts. "You are undisciplined. You don't sit your butt down in the chair and actually write for four hours at a time like real writers do."

Rather than whispering sweet nothings, Anxiety murmurs messages of fear and angst. "Are you sure your daughter is okay? Will she be able to keep her new job? Last one in, first one fired." Anxiety is the embodiment of Teddy Roosevelt's "Speak softly and carry a big stick" quote.

She makes appearances during daytime hours as well. And she's actually kind of glamorous, one of those femme fatale women of film noir fame in a form-fitting scarlet red dress, Charged-up-Cherry nail polish, and red lipstick. Longish dark wavy hair. Alexander McQueen heels. But instead of being an Ava Gardner, she is a Cruella de Vil.

So how do you dis-invite this unwanted, unwelcome visitor (who doesn't even have the good manners to knock?) Some of the obvious techniques are short-lived—wine, Xanax, exercise, wine. In fact, when the wine buzz wears off in the middle of the night, that's another time you wake up and find her sitting at the end of your bed, dropping ashes and venom on your newly dry-cleaned duvet.

As I crest toward seventy, I've grown accustomed to her visits. The length varies; sometimes her visits seem to last forever, and sometimes she just drops in and then leaves in a flash. As William Shakespeare observed, "Unbidden guests are often welcomest when they are gone".

Aside from reaching for wine and Xanax, how does one manage anxiety? Writing is a management technique that works for me. As Joan Didion said, "I don't know what I think until I write it down." Writing penetrates my mental mosh pit and provides clarity. As an avowed creativity evangelist, I believe creativity helps mitigate anxiety. Painting, sculpting, drawing, or creating music has a way of corralling your monkey chattering brain and meditatively focusing it on a creative expression project.

(Speaking of meditative, meditation is another good anxiety alleviator.)

I'm learning to live with anxiety's appearances, I just wish she'd choose a more convenient time to visit!

I DON'T WANT TO BE SOMEONE'S OXYGEN TANK

As noted in a previous chapter, I had knee replacement surgery. Following years of gel injections, cortisone shots, meniscus repair surgery, physical therapy, and lots and lots of ibuprofen, I couldn't take the pain, the limping, and bowlegs any longer. So I signed up for surgery. Friends and acquaintances used expressions such as "life changing" and "new lease on life" to describe the aftermath of this kind of surgery. I was optimistic. I guess because the post-surgery outcome is so good—the new knee renders the recipient capable of squatting like a toddler and hiking the Inca Trail—people don't bother to disclose how much the surgery HURTS! I also awoke with nerve damage causing foot drop (or "palsy"). The floppy foot was not my friend as I underwent physical therapy to rehab my knee. "This is really rare" was hardly the reassuring response I sought from my orthopedist, but it's the one I heard. Joint doctors, I've been told, are interpersonal eggplants.

I spent what felt like an endless night pushing the call button for the unfortunate nurse working the graveyard shift to help me, accompanied by my faithful IV pole, to the bathroom. Then there was Joint Boot Camp—a two-hour training session to introduce patients to basic physical therapy exercises—a requirement before I could be released from the hospital. I failed Joint Boot Camp. While my fellow campers were all sporting new hips and appeared to be zipping through the prescribed exercises, I refused to get out of my chair. "What is your pain level on a scale of 1 to 10?" we were asked. "Around two," several responded. (Ten being, "I feel like I'm crawling across broken glass naked.") I said, "Eight, and please give me another pain pill."

The Boot Camp commandant finally allowed me to leave camp and ultimately check out of the hospital. Since our townhouse is two-story with our master on the second floor, a hospital bed seemed to be a sleeping solution. Have you ever actually slept in a rented hospital bed? They are horrible. Climbing over the metal railings with my bum leg was excruciating. And, of course, I had to pee virtually every two hours. My devoted caregiver husband even slept on the sofa downstairs to keep tabs on my midnight walker-wanderings.

Okay, so I think I have accurately, albeit dramatically, set the stage for my state of misery during my post-surgery stint. But did my misery and worry over my dangling foot deter people from pulling at my suffering psyche for their own benefit? That would be a big *no*.

A dear family member, accustomed to relying on me as her oxygen tank, was confronted with yet another crisis. And this family member, bless her heart, does not suffer in silence. Not when she can unload her anxiety onto me. I gently reminded her of my brokenness, which was met with, "Oh, I'm so sorry. That is awful. What can I do to help?" The sincere-sounding sympathy lasted five minutes and then, "Now, back to me."

Recognizing my limited emotional bandwidth, my husband stepped up to the rescue. Crisis averted, I had to grudgingly laugh during a phone call with said family member when she said, "My boss sucks, but I'm really loving all this family bonding time." Oy vey! #thelifeofareluctantangel.

BBLB Manual of Maxims #29:
"Avoid becoming someone's oxygen tank."

RELATIONSHIPS SHOULD BE A TENNIS MATCH

I read a 2018 *Wall Street Journal* article entitled, "Baby Boomers Get More Selective About Friends." According to the article, baby boomers are less socially engaged than people the same age were twenty years ago.[1]

There are several theories emerging about this phenomenon: (1) Many boomers are still working, (2) Boomers are caring for aging parents, leaving less time to visit with friends, (3) Lady Boomers are assuming more child care duties for grandchildren, and (4) technology and social media (which were not accessible twenty years ago) often take the place of physical interactions.

Laura Carstensen, director of the Stanford Center on Longevity, was quoted in the *WSJ* article saying she engages socially only with a small circle of family and friends. She said,

> *"I certainly find myself being more selective. Neighbors and friends don't just stop by the house the way they did when I was growing up. Now when I hear the doorbell, especially at night and if alone, it's almost alarming."*

The pollster in me just had to conduct a quiz of Boomer women to determine whether they were becoming more selective about the relationships they're willing to maintain and burn calories for. The results were consistent with the findings in the *WSJ* article. Fifty-seven percent said they had fewer relationships they were willing to maintain compared to twenty years ago. Seventy-two percent agreed with the following statement: *Since there are only fifty-two weekends in a year, I want to spend them with people I really care about and who care about me.*

While there are downsides to aging, an upside is the fact we get more selective about our relationships. When I was growing up, I got the message from my mother I was supposed to be popular. I suspect, given the hardships she endured in her young years, this was a longing she transferred to her only daughter. And, like the responsible first-born child that I am, I've carried around that unspoken mandate for years. Advanced age, however, has made me question those one-sided relationships. If it's not a tennis match in which the emotional and conversational volleys go back and forth, is it worth it to stay in the relationship at all? (I love that metaphor, given to me by a dear friend struggling with these same questions).

BBLB RECAP

What do reluctant angels, trash cans, and oxygen tanks have in common? They serve as waste repositories and life support systems. Goodness and generosity are at the root of angel actions. But angels, if abused, can become reluctant and recalcitrant. Assuming others' anxieties can overburden them, causing them to cash in their angel careers or morph into martyrs. The world needs the angels among us. So before maxing out, try the following survival techniques: (1) impose a weight limit on the amount of debris deposits allowed in your trash can; (2) unless someone is willing to reciprocate and share oxygen tanks, limit your face time with them; (3) try to identify healthier strategies for managing anxiety rather than allowing (her, him, it) to hijack your dreams and awakenings; and (4) going forward, invest only in relationships that are two-sided. It's not worth the calorie burn to exist in a one-sided relationship.

I've been skirting around the B word in this chapter. Boundaries. Establishing boundaries is tough. It's like trying to train a dog; hard to be consistent, but worth the effort to have a non-barking, non-jumping, non-crazy canine. This is, of course, easier said than done. I have two jumping, biting, barking canines, so boundary setting is not my strong suit. But I'm committed to trying.

EXERCISE YOUR CREATIVITY #7:

LET'S SERVE AS GOD'S PROXIES

Instead of becoming a reluctant angel, try serving as God's proxy. In my thirty-plus years in the political business, I've never encountered such a lack of civility and, worse yet, empathy as I've experienced in the past ten years. I've witnessed many people retreat into their bubbles of sameness, choosing to associate with people of the same color, ethnicity, religion, and political views. I confess to my culpability on this front as well. I don't think there is anyone among my "friends" on Facebook with whom I disagree.

So, in light of this divisiveness, I'm actively seeking opportunities to connect with people who have racial and income differences from me. I've also been working with an arts initiative designed to offer creative expression programming to under-served youth. Art is a great way to bridge differences.

The upshot? I'm enjoying these exchanges with my fellow humans. This mission probably sounds obvious. Of course, this is what we should do, and I know so many of you are already behaving in this manner. But I think it has grown increasingly easy to isolate ourselves within our comfortable communities and bury our attention in our smart phones.

"Let's Serve As God's Proxies" is a line I stumbled upon. While I don't consider myself to be overly religious, I like the implication of the phrase. Consider choosing one or or two subgroups whose members are different from you perhaps due to: ➤

- Racial or ethnic differences
- Language barriers and country of origin differences
- Social and economic differences
- Age differences
- Political differences
- Occupational differences
- Physical differences

How might an atheist approach an evangelical? Can a carpenter connect with a chemical engineer or a lawyer with a landscaper? Do we tend to avoid people with noticeable physical differences? (Thin and heavy; tattooed or not; wheelchair restricted or a marathon runner.) The list of opportunities is as extensive as the number of people in our universe. Use your skills and talents to form connections, or even just start by saying hello in recognition of your mutual humanity. I think even these little acts of acknowledgement and kindness can count as serving as God's proxies in the world. And just maybe, if we're all a little kinder, people will take over responsibility for their own trash and oxygen.

BBLB Manual of Maxims #30:
"Let's serve as God's proxies."

CHAPTER 8:

Great-Grand Parenting

"Never have children, just grandchildren."
—GORE VIDAL

I tend to believe baby boomers got the memo outlining the requisite qualifications for being devoted grandparents. My experience and that of many of my friends suggests good grandparenting behavior skipped a generation or two. I was a grandchild at one point in my life having had remote relationships with grandparents who lived far away—maybe we saw them once a year, and telephone conversations were rare given the cost of long-distance calls. My brothers and I would receive cards at Christmas and birthdays with a note saying that our present, usually five dollars, was being deposited into a savings account for us. The money came in handy when at eighteen, I had six hundred dollars to buy my first car, but what kid enjoys delayed gratification for eighteen years? My children also had grandparents—just not the doting, babysitting, indulgent kind.

I was sixty by the time my first grandchild was born. I am now the grandmother of three, two boys and a girl. Being a grandparent is like eating an ice cream sundae every day with no calorie penalties. It's delicious. "It's the only thing that is *not* underrated," I heard prior to my tenure as a doting grandma. Not everyone has the biological opportunity to be a grandparent. Nevertheless, it is a role that can be fulfilled in other ways if the desire is there. Two of my little ones live twelve hundred miles away, and to compensate for their absence, I volunteer as a foster grandparent at a Boys & Girls Club in downtown Orlando. "Grands," as we're called, provide much needed one-on-one time with kids whose parents are often working two and three jobs to provide for their families. Nurturing young ones on the path to becoming fully functioning humans is a worthy pursuit.

I do, however, have a bone to pick with Google and Madison Avenue. How in the world are we supposed to maintain our sass when we're characterized as decrepit little old ladies with unattractive hair and canes? Foraging for images, I kept coming upon wrinkled, crippled creatures barely resembling human beings. My offense at these depictions probably has something to do with recognizing my own facial crevices and sagging neck. Oh God, the neck! Even a quick glance in the mirror tells me mine resembles a turkey's wattle. I FaceTime often with my grandchildren and am horrified at the way I look on these exchanges. The wattle, the double chin. What must they think of me?

How do we manage the juxtaposition of our physical changes with enjoying our sought-after grandparenting gig? You rock the look—that's how. You behave in such a way that your biological or foster children and grandchildren will believe every one of your lines and wrinkles is beautiful. Following the GRP (Grandmother's Rules of Procedure) guidelines can help achieve that goal: (1) Shine a light for your kids and provide a perspective on parenting; (2) Be Useful (3) Lightly skirt parental rules and mandates/be indulgent (4) Don't play the guilt card; (5) Keep your mouth shut. Keep your anxieties and opinions to yourself or share them with friends; and last but far from least (6) Be an advocate for yourself because grandmothering can be taxing on the body.

BBLB Manual of Maxims #31:
"Following the GRP Guidelines will sass up your role as grandmother."

GRP #1: SHINE A LIGHT

Even if parts of us are dimming, grandparents are perfectly positioned to shine a light for their families, even if it's only a flashlight. Parenting is fraught with responsibility and anxiety. Once men and women assume that parental yoke of responsibility, they become nearsighted, often able to see only three feet in front of them. But grandparents have the luxury of an aerial view.

"He'll be fine," we reassure them.

"Kids are resilient. He won't remember this slight next week."

"She's just acting out because of the new baby."

"Don't worry—she's a lovely girl and will find her own group of friends in school who will appreciate her."

The grandparent's experience, if offered without judgement, can guide their child-parent out of the darkness. It's a valuable role.

My mother died when my daughter was three and my son was nine months, so they never really knew her. My first mother-in-law violated many of the Grandmother Rules of Procedure guidelines. I invited Elaine to stay in my home following the birth of my daughter, and I regretted that decision within hours. In hindsight, I recognize her own anxieties permeated every criticism.

"You shouldn't nurse her! She's not gaining weight. She's not getting enough nourishment." Breastfeeding was hard enough but having someone standing over my shoulder admonishing me was brutal.

"I think David has an eating disorder!" My son was ten at the time. He was and remains a picky eater. I didn't need her fears thrust in my face; I had enough of my own. I needed her to comfort me, to tell me everything was going to be okay, to hold my baby when I was sleep deprived from getting up three times each night—*not* tell me what I was doing wrong.

My experience as a daughter-in-law taught me a lesson: as a mother and grandmother, I need to keep my mouth shut. Lady Boomers are not known for keeping their opinions to themselves, so what should we do with all those pent-up opinions? Share them with friends.

One holiday season following the birth of my oldest grandson, I realized I had become a member of a Grandmother's Network. I was included in a text thread initiated by my friend Grace and our cadre of grandmother friends. Her one-year-old great niece was visiting for Christmas and Grace needed to equip her home with kid stuff. The following is the gist of how this exchange went down:

Jackie: I have a highchair
Liz: I have an umbrella stroller
Cynthia: I have a Little Tikes Cozy Coupe riding car
Liz: I have a portable crib
Betsy: I have a pack and play
Ann: I have lots of toys
Nancy: I have books

We had amassed these trinkets for tots from rummage sales, Costco purchases, and inheritances from grand-friends whose own tots had transitioned into much bigger kids. Baby boomer women, being the basic parental overachievers that we are, want to ensure our nests are ready and accommodating for those hard-earned grandbabies. Our band of boomer grandmothers participate in our own version of a sharing economy. We also share our "eye rolling" tales about overanxious daughters and daughters-in-law who allow only organic, free range, grass fed, all-natural food to pass over the lips of our princes and princesses. Far more judicious to share eye rolls with friends than the parents.

GRP #2: BE USEFUL

Aside from shining a light, baby boomer grandparents can be useful. We often have flexible schedules that allow us to help with childcare, and Lady Boomers have a great deal of empathy for the plight of working parents. I clearly remember how difficult it was to find and keep good babysitters, and I can remember only a few occasions when my father and his wife stepped up to help with my kids. Hard lesson learned, and I vowed to be helpful to my family. After all, no outsider loves those precious miracles more than we do. So when our kids send out the SOS, we dust off our superhero grandma capes, hop in a car or on a plane, and ride to the rescue.

Lesley Stahl discussed her book, *Becoming Grandma: The Joys and Science of the New Grandparenting*, during a 2016 episode of *CBS Sunday Morning* entitled, "Boomer Grandparents Play Mom and Dad Part-Time."

The definition of being a grandmother is pure joy, unconditional love. Loving them for who they are not what we want them to be. Not loving them for what jobs they are going to have, just the mere joy of being in the same space with them.[1]

Stahl noted that the cost of childcare often exceeds the cost of college and noted that boomer parents are stepping in to help. She interviewed former president of Wheaton College, Tish Emerson, whom she dubbed a "granny nanny" for twin grandchildren. Emerson serves an essential role in the lives of her grandchildren, taking them to skating practice, feeding them, and offering her apartment for homework time. As a busy college president, she says she missed many of these experiences with her own children. Emerson confessed she needs her grandchildren as much as they need her. She wrote,

It's a chance to see things develop with your grandchildren you were unable to do with your own kids, working full time. It's kind of a second life, a second chance. When you are a working parent, time is your enemy. When you are a grandparent, time is different, and you are able to be more relaxed.

I have dubbed baby boomers the "Tweener Generation," sandwiched between parenting adult children and caring for aging parents. Now we're taking care of our grandchildren, so that means baby boomers have been and are caregivers to three generations, sometimes simultaneously. Caring for this latest generation, I suspect, will be the most fun. Lady Boomer grandmothers beware, however. Our aging bodies can pay a price for those caregiving services.

HELP! UBER SAVE ME

I was invited to serve as a childminder for my Chicago-area grandchildren for a week one summer. My son and his wife were without a babysitter and their therapy schedules were chock-full with clients.

I was bound and determined the week would be full of adventures for our threesome (Maya then three, Ru one, and me, sixty-five). Day one found us at the Chicago Botanical Gardens. The gardens were brimming with stunning flowers with names like the Plum Fantasy Rose and the tiny Countess Carrot. A garden devoted to butterflies occupied most of our time. I really came to understand the origin of "butterfly kisses" as those delicate creatures lightly caressed Ru's cheeks and hair.

A model railroad featuring miniature trains running on 1,600 feet of tracks through handcrafted vignettes of American scenes and icons took up the remainder of our time. Afterward, I took the long way home down beautiful Sheridan Road flanked by gracious mansions, allowing sleepy children to take postponed naps.

Day two found us at the Lincoln Park Zoo trying mightily to awaken sleeping lions and howler monkeys napping in the noon-day sun. There were exotic birds, flamingos, one giraffe, and two zebras, and best of all—a cherry Italian ice that found more of itself on Maya's dress than on her tongue.

4:30 found me pushing a stroller and negotiating our exit with a very determined and sticky three-year-old. We were one hot, tired, cranky bunch by the time we reached our car. I should have known when the remote would not open the door we were in trouble. And yes, of course, the car would not start. Panic engulfed my solar plexus as one child restlessly ran after geese in the adjacent park and the other struggled to extract himself from the stroller.

The parents, in the middle of counseling sessions, were virtually unreachable. AAA was two hours away and I knew that by the time they arrived my little ones would be swimming in the lake with the waterfowl they had chased into the water. "HELP! Uber, I need you!" My female knight in shining armor arrived shortly in her red Dodge Durango.

As I contemplated the transfer of car seats from one car to the other, I pleaded with my granddaughter, "I'll buy you anything you want at Target if you stay put and watch Ruie." And when, by the way, was the last time you hoisted a car seat?! They weigh at least twenty-five pounds empty, they're extremely cumbersome, and disengaging them calls for an engineering degree (as does reinstalling them). Millennial parents are passionate about car seat safety, so I felt incredible pressure to make sure my grandchildren were bolted securely in the Durango. Fortunately, my KISA (Knight in Shining Armor) had experience with car seats, although she refused to allow the pound of whole wheat goldfish lodged in the car seats to travel with the children. (The parking lot near our car resembled a dry koi pond.)

One hour later (because the Uber driver went south instead of north on Lakeshore Drive, embroiling us in 5:00 p.m. Chicago traffic) we arrived home. And of course, both children were sound asleep. Again, the panic. "How do I lift my sleeping forty-five-pound granddaughter, her twenty-five-pound brother, and two car seats?" Fortunately, my knight in shining armor came to my rescue yet again, following me to the front porch with car seats in tow. I gave my savior a five-star rating and a good tip. Parents weren't due home for another three hours, which meant I was responsible for dinner and bath time. (My son and I had to meet AAA downtown to resuscitate the abandoned Subaru, which took another two hours.) I crawled into bed that night totally wiped! It took me two days before I could even refer to the zoo playdate as "joyful exhaustion." I wouldn't trade the experience for anything, but it's easy for our fatigue to gobble up our color. Even though the spirit is willing, the body may have reservations. So we must be our own advocates. That experience taught me two bodies are better than one. My husband accompanies me now on these rescue missions.

I NAILED KINDERGARTEN

The number one complaint I heard from my Lady Boomer friends during the pandemic was about their inability to spend time with their grandchildren (oh and yes, staying healthy was a concern, too.) I knew just how they felt. Nine months had elapsed between visits with my Chicago family. So after months of negotiation amid the raging virus, my husband and I managed to score a trip north to see our kids and grandchildren. Negotiation is the operative word here, as trip after trip was postponed by fear of Covid contamination from airline travel.

We suspected that our fifteen-day stay would not really be a vacation but more of a rescue mission. Our kids were exhausted. They had been running their tele-therapy business from their home office, acting as teaching assistants for virtual kindergarten, and maintaining some semblance of a household.

We opted for a hotel stay since "our" room had been converted to a classroom for virtual kindergarten. We tried to be the consummate guests, arriving each morning at 9:00 a.m. carrying Starbucks pumpkin cream cold brews for the adults and cake pops for afternoon kid treats. Then our workday would commence as teaching assistant for my kindergartener and babysitter for the three-year-old.

It had been a long time since I had to help with kinder-garten assignments. Each morning Maya and I would take our seats in the child-sized chairs at her activity table, and she would sign on to Zoom for her morning circle session. I was amazed at this five-year old's proficiency with the Zoom app. I knew adults who took fifteen minutes trying to access the program. So right out of the box, I was a proud grandmother.

The school day consisted of thirty-minute sessions interspersed with short pauses for potty breaks and work assignments. I was glued to her color-coded schedule (which changed each day of the week), nervous I would miss a session or assignment. While I might have had per-formance anxiety, the work was interspersed with so many good parts. Pappy, a.k.a. grandfather Jim, was enlisted as Ru's personal playmate. A giant Hot Wheels garage equipped with a car-eating T-Rex dinosaur occupied much of their day along with dodge ball in the backyard bouncy house. I got to be a fly on the wall observing my five-year-old granddaughter mute and unmute herself participating with eight others in a kindergarten experience I barely recognized. I was privy to her classroom insights as she occasionally rolled her eyes, talking out of one side of her mouth (a facial expression I've seen from her mother on many occasions) commenting, "Abby and Bailey like to talk a lot!" Her spot-on analysis and conscientious behavior was so reminiscent of her perceptive parents. I was filled with pride as she grasped concepts like *more than and less than* in her ST Math independent sessions.

But I felt I was on a real seesaw trying to figure out what button would take me to which assignment posted by the teacher on an app called Seesaw. The process was quite a challenge!

Monday (after work) on the fifteenth day, my husband and I took our leave to return home. Many tears flowed but also some humor as I said to my daughter-in-law, "Katie, after two weeks I've nailed this kindergarten thing!"

"Now you really get me, Liz Kitchens," she replied. It was an honor to share burdens that felt as light as clouds.

Flying home, I felt a surprisingly large weight lift from my shoulders. I felt free (as one can be on an airplane) to read, write, and nap. I was free to return to my life. But nestled there between my ribs was a warm contentment from sharing in the lives of my loved ones. I was useful. I was needed. I was joyfully exhausted.

GRP #3: SKIRT THE RULES, INDULGE YOUR GRANDCHILDREN

Why do grandchildren and grandparents get along so well? They have a common enemy. Households are mini governments with rules and ordinances that need to be enacted and obeyed in order to function in the real world, and these governments are rarely democratically run. Parents are the governors and the kids the citizens, and while the citizens often stage rebellions, the parents still wield the power. Grandparents, years removed from their despotic days, tend to ally with the citizens. Maybe it's a way of getting even with our kids for their torturous rebellions against us.

Grandparents are in the enviable position of lightly skirting those pesky parental edicts. They can say yes when parents keep having to say no. "Yes, you can stay up past your bedtime." "Yes, I'll buy you that Minecraft video game for your switch." "Yes, sweetheart, of course you can have another cookie. Do you want some ice cream too?" Obviously, this is not the "shiner of the light" aspect of grandparenting, but it's fun getting to say yes.

Even though the pandemic limited access to grandchildren, many grandparents compensated by playing remote Mrs. Santa Claus. (No wonder Jeff Bezos was able to buy his own rocket company and blast into outer space. Amazon made a fortune during the pandemic delivering necessities and grandparent treats.) We wanted to stay relevant. When his mother refused to buy him an expensive toy one day during the pandemic, Ru replied, "Well, Jozy (my grandmother name) will buy it for me." Uh oh, I should include yet another rule in the grandmother's playbook: Even though it's OK to skirt a few rules and be indulgent, don't get into a contest with mom.

Your grandparent credentials can be stripped from you in a heartbeat. Speaking of contests and indulgences . . .

As I've mentioned, two of my grandchildren live "away," as they say, in Maine—1,180 miles away in Evanston, Illinois to be precise (and maybe just a little bit bitter.) My grandson Austin lives much closer, just thirty-two miles away. But while it's obviously more difficult to see the Chicago clan, somehow even driving an hour in snarled traffic on Interstate 4, the main north and south corridor traveling through Central Florida, has resulted in not enough in-person time with Austin.

One day I proposed to my husband that we conduct a campaign. After all, campaigns have been our jam for more than thirty years. We help candidates develop communications strategies to win votes. Why couldn't we employ some of those same skills to communicate with people we love? We decided to take a retro approach to our campaign and employed the postal service to deliver periodic care packages to Maya, Austin, and Ru. And they absolutely love receiving packages and notes in their mailboxes.

Aside from little gift treats, we collect:

- fun postcards featuring animals sharing fun facts, travel scenery, children's illustrator art, postcards, and even Florida attractions.
- fun stamps of Thomas the Train, Snoopy, and characters from *Frozen* and *Toy Story*.
- items that we purchased while travelling, including Russian nesting dolls, a kaleidoscope, and handmade German ornaments.

Yes, I admit it, just like trying to win the hearts and minds of voters, I have been on a mission to win the hearts and minds of my little ones. And rest assured, I have not allowed the Russians or anyone else to interfere in this election campaign.

And what is the reward for adhering to the rules in the grandmother's handbook? We get to gorge ourselves with the calorie-free deliciousness of those babies. I remember the first time Maya came to visit over a Memorial Day weekend (Oh, and yes, her parents came too.)

I was bedazzled by the fact our four-month-old granddaughter could:

- sit up (with a great deal of propping and assistance thanks to those foam Bumbo chairs).
- hold her head up, albeit in a bobble head fashion.
- respond with such a wide mouthed smile my heart performed somersaults like a cartoon acrobat.
- gurgle laugh when her neck was tickled or even when the dog barked.
- talk in a husky cooing voice.

Those advances represented a major change since visiting her the first month of her life when her only skill set was preventing her parents from sleeping.

Each morning during her Memorial Day weekend visit, the bedroom door would open and the two of them would emerge. Her father in boxers, and Maya in a diaper, a mass of exposed flesh and dangling limbs. "Here, I'm going back to bed," Dad would say, plopping her and a pack of diapers into my arms. Those mornings ticked off at least a couple of the boxes in the GRP. I was useful, enabling her parents to get some much-needed sleep, and I could indulge her with my undivided attention for two hours. And I was rewarded mightily during these delicious exchanges. Brother Time suspended himself during the ensuing two hours as we engaged in "motherese" (a.k.a baby talk), hugs, and baby games. I was in heaven.

A day, a month, and a year before Maya was born (but who's keeping track), Austin, our first grandchild, came into our world. Austin is the first born of my stepson, Jamie. Jamie has a mom and a mother-in-law with whom his little family is quite close, so I fretted over my place in the grandmother hierarchy. Step relationships can be complicated. Gazing into his two-day-old eyes, however, I knew I would fight mightily for a significant role in his life. His heart doesn't seem to discriminate between natural and step grandparents. He accepts all the love (and presents) and pours it back with equal abandon. It's actually a revelation that those artificial biological lines are irrelevant in the grandparent/grandchild relationship, a fact for which I am utterly grateful.

MY GRANDSON SHOWED ME THE LIGHT

How many times have you said or heard someone say, "Don't you just love fall?" I remember Meg Ryan in *You've Got Mail* talking about how much she loved New York in the fall. Living in Florida we get the "You don't really have discernible seasons" rap, as if to say, "You have no concept of fall. The 'real' fall only happens north of you." Well, I beg to disagree. Our leaves change color, albeit ever so slightly. After months spent running from an air-conditioned house to an air-conditioned car to an air-conditioned office avoiding the oppressive heat and humidity, it's fun to be outside. The quality of the light changes. And we get to decorate for Halloween. It tickles one's spirit to behold patches of pumpkins perched on porches and witches wrapping their arms around trees, not to mention those fun orange lights illuminating shrubs and doorways.

One year, just before Halloween, I was excited to invite my stepson, daughter-in-law, and our then almost two-year-old grandson over for a Sunday stroll to look at lights and Halloween decorations. Our gang of four adults, two dogs, and one little boy pushing a stroller set out for the tour. I was like an ADHD four-year-old excitedly pointing out clusters of orange lights here and purple lights over there. Mildly interested, Austin kept pointing upward saying "Moon, moon," as the almost full orb dipped in and out of the clouds. "Yes, that's really cool Austin. But look over there at the funny pumpkin faces."

"Moon," he persisted. And we all finally paused to behold the miracle of the moon. The light emanating from the moon illuminated the sky and our pathway. It truly was much more beautiful than the fake lights wrapped around bushes and porch railings. As the grownups in the world, we spend a lot of time rushing around doing *stuff*. Austin showed me the light that evening as we paused to be mindful of the moon and all its glory. Number one in the grandmother's guidebook urges us to shine the light for our kids. It's often the case our grandchildren reveal the light for us as well. Lesson learned that night.

GRP #4: AVOID PLAYING THE VICTIM CARD

Want to know what would exponentially improve the image of grandparents and parents? Not playing the victim card with our kids and grandkids. The parents of baby boomers didn't hesitate to play the "poor me" game, which reminds me of a joke going around when my children were young:

> *"How many grandmothers does it take to change a lightbulb?*
> *"None. It's ok, I'll just sit in the dark."*

Guilt is a manipulative weapon and almost as damaging as a physical weapon. And it is tempting to employ. "After all we've done for you!" This complaint assumes the parent/child relationship is a transactional one. "I spent so much money supporting you, you owe me." Even if we don't actually say those words, we probably think them, at least once a day. I suspect any decent therapist would advise avoiding this transactional view of parenting.

The holidays are often occasions when the guilt card is played. "Oh, I see. You're taking the kids to spend Christmas with their *other* grandparents," we say, breathing guilt, disappointment, and disapproval into the cell phone exchange. And it's true, spending the holidays and special occasions without our kids and/or grandchildren can be tough. It is incumbent upon us, however, to recognize that our kids are entitled to make plans of their own. And those plans, especially as grandchildren grow older, may not include us. As much as I try to remember this, there are occasions when I dread the prospect.

One Thanksgiving, post-pandemic, I was having blue expectations about the looming Thanksgiving holiday. Our kids had planned their own celebrations, and I had to work hard to keep the disappointment out of my voice and facial expressions on FaceTime. I truly did not want to guilt them into including us in their holiday plans. Instead, I moped around my house and overshared my feelings with friends. Writing about my blue expectations in my journal helped. I realized I needed to re-frame my view and attitudes. And, as it turned out, blessings scattered themselves throughout the Thanksgiving week.

The first stop on my gratitude train came on Tuesday of Thanksgiving week when our grandson, Austin, came for a slumber party. We decorated our Christmas tree and explored neighborhood Christmas lights after dark. Just being in proximity to this thoughtful, loving little boy was emotionally nourishing. As it turned out, who cares if the event is celebrated on Tuesday versus Thursday?

Wednesday's stop deposited my husband and me in New Smyrna Beach, Florida for four days of gorgeous, seventy-degree weather. The soothing voice of the ocean washed away any prospect of sadness from our solo holiday status.

Our Thanksgiving Day stop brought a delightful interaction among family members. My daughter, granddaughter, and I celebrated a virtual Thanksgiving via the Animal Crossing game on our Nintendo Switches. My Nintendo Switch was given to me as a birthday present during the pandemic and has enabled me to enjoy family time online. Holidays are a big deal in the Animal Crossing world. Tracy and I flew on our respective seaplanes to Peritucci, Maya's Island paradise. Maya's animal creature neighbors milled about the plaza in the town center. Tom the turkey prepared the Thanksgiving meal. Villagers and visitors took part in a scavenger hunt, searching for key ingredients for Tom's special recipes. "I need three manilla clams and one scallop for my famous clam chowder," he instructed our threesome, "and I need one orange and one white pumpkin to prepare my world-famous pumpkin pie." Off our characters scrambled around the island in pursuit of ingredients. As much as I adore a good scavenger hunt, the fact that I was participating in this event with my daughter and granddaughter was my favorite part of this exchange. We connected on two fronts—virtually through the Nintendo Switch and live via our Zoom apps. It was so much fun! I laughed until my stomach was sore. Maya's Animal Crossing expertise far exceeds that of her aunt's and grandmother's. My husband was hooting as he overheard our granddaughter patiently guiding us in navigating her island.

It wasn't a typical Thanksgiving. I didn't get to kiss Maya's cherubic cheeks or hug my daughter, but nevertheless, it was a point of connection and joy. I guess connections come in all different forms and shapes. And I, for one, was very thankful. I was also rewarded with an airline ticket to spend the week between Christmas and New Year's with my kids that year.

BBLB Manual of Maxims # 32:
"Instead of playing the guilt card, play the reframing card. It's transformative."

GRANDCHILDREN ARE MIRACLE HEALERS

Yet another reward for following the GRP formula is the healing capabilities of grandchildren.

Following complications from knee replacement surgery, I took my self-pitying self to Chicago for a vacation. My melancholy moping lasted perhaps a half hour around the then four-year-old Maya and two-year-old Ru. They expressed curiosity about the nature of my boo boo, even offering their medical expertise and toy stethoscope for further examination. But then it was, "Enough about you, Jozy, let's get back to me." Their attitudes, I'm convinced, helped speed my recovery because I couldn't dwell on my own disappointments. In order to have a successful relationship with grandkids, the adults in the room must be mindful of the "No Selfish Zone" surrounding children. Their needs trump ours, as well they should.

MY NAME IS JOZY

My name has changed several times over the years. I started out as Linda Lang but spent one too many years in school enduring the "Are you Superman's girlfriend" taunts. You might remember Lois Lane, writer and cub reporter, and Lana Lang, the other woman in the Superman saga. So, at the age of twenty-one, at the juncture of changing cities and moving to a new life, I dropped the Linda in favor of my middle name, Elizabeth, which I felt and still feel fits me. To me, "Liz" sounds zippy, which is the way I feel inside. Then there were the marriages resulting in name changes. #whyintheworlddidInotkeepmymaidenname!

Linda Lang morphed into Liz Lang and then Liz Hauser for twelve or so years, followed by a remarriage adding the name Kitchens to my nomenclature repertoire. At the point of my re-marriage, I considered taking back my OG name since I would have to undergo countless bureaucratic name changes anyway. But that just caused more angst. "Then there would be *three* different last names among five people in our household," I wailed to my then fiancé. So, I adopted Kitchens, the third major iteration of my name.

The name omitted from the above list but the one of which I'm most proud is Jozy. I received that designation in 2015 from my then new granddaughter. FaceTime is the best when grandchildren live more than a thousand miles away. Apparently, my Labradoodle Jozy thought so too and occupied more than a few of the FaceTime frames. Maya would point and squeal at the dog. Somehow, the association became my new name, Jozy (Our family has a history of naming people after pets. Maya's brother was named Rusty in honor of their first Labradoodle).

During a President's Day weekend trip to Chicago, I was invited to visit Maya's newish social sphere, her pre-school classroom. I was a guest teacher leading a clay Valentine's Arts and Crafts project (arts and craps as her adorable brother called it.) I was so excited and nervous, I prepped for hours rolling out clay and cutting out heart shapes. Maya introduced me to friends and invited me to join circle and snack time. Her almond-shaped hazel eyes registered a measure of surprise when she looked up at me saying, "They like you, Jozy!" Never have I been prouder of a name than I was that day. It was the ultimate reward for my imperfect attempts at adhering to the grandmother's procedure manual.

BBLB RECAP

Whether biological or foster, grandchildren are one of the only experiences in this life that *aren't* overrated. How do we go about being a great grandparent (without having to start at eighteen having children)? Follow the GRP (Grandmother's Rules of Procedure) formula outlined in this chapter. Doing so will elicit such gratitude and adoration your loved ones won't notice your floppy folds and drooping eyelids. Remember these guidelines:

- **Shine a light for your children.** Remind them most spats and injuries are temporary. The sun will come up tomorrow.
- **Be useful.** Help when you can. Your anxious, sleep-deprived kids will be grateful.
- **Be indulgent.** Small treats go a long way. Adapt to their level. When they're babies physically get down to their level to look them in the eyes and make them laugh. When they're older, buy the video games they love. While you're at it, buy a game system for yourself so you can play together when they visit. When they're older, take an interest in their music choices. Make your gifts fun, targeted, and thoughtful.
- **Avoid playing the guilt card.** Don't behave as if you're a victim. The goal is to behave in such a way children and grandchildren want to spend time with you, not feel they have to.
- **Keep your mouth shut.** Don't second guess the parenting decisions of your kids. And whenever possible, avoid sharing your own anxieties about the grandchildren.

- **Don't sacrifice yourself.** Your body is aging. We do have digestive issues and arthritic knees. It's real. Hoisting those heavy car seats and little ones compromises us physically. The day my youngest grandchild was born, my granddaughter and I happily danced and pranced all over downtown Chicago, to the extent I managed to fracture my knee. Pain can zap our sass.

I am not suggesting that you be perfect in the execution of these steps. Far from it. Striving for perfection is another one of those Boomer behaviors that erode our color and zap our sass. Just be open and try a couple. Their responses will reward your efforts.

EXERCISE YOUR CREATIVITY #8:

BECOME A FAIRY GRANDPARENT

As Covid played havoc with our health, it also hindered our ability to spend time with our grandchildren. Having to decide between spending time with children and grandchildren and staying safe at home felt like Sophie's Choice. Plane trips and hotel stays were required to visit long distance relatives. "I have grandchildren withdrawal," wailed a friend accustomed to spending days each week with her threesome.

Two friends crafted a strategy to mitigate their misery. They identified neighborhood little ones missing out on their own grandparents. Nancy took to hiding little treasures in the bushes and on the cobblestone path leading to her front door. Each morning her three- and five-year-old neighbors delighted in scouring her shrubs and steps for the colorful gems and stones left by fairies. Ann painted rocks and snuck them across the street to be found by the resident two-year-old. She also quilted baby blankets for a new grandniece and nephew.

To be human is to crave connection. Connecting with young ones is a joyous way to satisfy that craving regardless of whether you are a biological grandparent or not. And parents need you. They are struggling. Managing a career, household responsibilities, often playing teacher's assistant in virtual school sessions. Find a safe way to help. I'm certain many of you are already doing this but just in case you need help:

- Give parents a break. Spend time with their kids, offer to babysit, create crafts, help with homework.
- Kids love receiving mail. Send fun postcards decorated with fun and interesting stamps.
- Bake goodies or drop off a meal. Food is always a welcome treat for families.
- Create your own magic. Hide treasures in their yard or yours. Their delight will be your own.

CHAPTER 9:

Caregivers Living in Color

*"How porous the border is between the sick and the well . . .
As we live longer . . . a majority of us will travel back and forth
across these realms. The idea of striving for some beautiful,
perfect state of wellness? It mires us in eternal dissatisfaction,
a goal forever out of reach. To be well now is to learn to accept
whatever body and mind I currently have."*
—SULEIKA JAOUAD

As a baby boomer married to an even older baby boomer, I'm convinced many of us will face caregiving duties. Now, you might say, "I am or have already cared for an aging parent." Others might say, "I'm integral to the care of my grandchildren." And still another might add, "I'm caring for an aging parent *and* my grandchildren."

Caring for others has kind of been the MO of our generation, particularly for women. We have been hyper involved in the care of our kids, including our adult kids. More than one-third of Boomers have simultaneously supported and cared for older and younger family members. As noted in chapter two, the Boomer Generation can truly be dubbed the "Tweener Generation," sandwiched as we have been between parenting adult children and caring for aging parents.

It's a good thing our generation enjoyed sex, drugs, and rock-in-roll in our youth because our adulthood has and will be fraught with a considerable amount of responsibility. While I know we are up to the challenge, I wonder if we have really paused to consider how we feel about caring for our spouse/partner?

I have few, if any, Florence Nightingale attributes. When my children were young, I could barely stay in the same room with their vomit. I didn't know where their vomiting ended, and my gagging began. My husband (their stepdad) and his robust constitution came to the rescue, stripping the bed and cleaning the toilet.

Since 1984, self-reproach has dogged me for failing to provide more emotional support for my mom prior to her death. I dutifully cared for her basic needs but averted my eyes from her oozing wound and wanted to plug my ears to her wracking coughs. The role reversal was painful. I wish I had snuggled more with her or read to her from a favorite book.

Money solves a lot of these issues. If you are flush with cash, someone else can handle the yucky, laborious parts of caregiving. If not, those responsibilities will probably land in your lap. And we can become reluctant angels. Few of us look forward to this day. We don't want our lives to change. We value our freedom of movement and independence. But as Suleika Jaouad says in her 2021 book, *Between Two Kingdoms,* we will suffer disappointment and dissatisfaction if we spend our time seeking that perfect state of wellness.[1] The goal is acceptance of whatever state our mind and body occupy in the present moment. To some, this attitude sounds passive, but quite the opposite is true. Acceptance is an active state of mind, and it's brave. Creative thinking comes to our rescue. Thinking creatively about this phase will help inform our attitudes about the process. Our Magenta can shine vibrantly in this newish phase of life.

THE PARADOX OF CAREGIVING

Caregiving comes in all shapes and forms. It's stressful, time-consuming, and exhausting. But curiously, sprinkled in with the stress, is intimacy. One February I found myself in the role of caregiver, and my charges were on opposite ends of the age spectrum. The first stint was in Chicago, caring for two- and four-year-old grandchildren. On the heels of that caregiving gig, my husband underwent sinus surgery, the recovery from which took about four weeks. As I mentioned, Florence Nightingale I'm not, but I managed to change bandages and ice packs and perform my household jobs along with his.

Changing dirty diapers and bloody bandages, I was struck by the intimacy intrinsic to this level of caring. Human beings are full of contradictions. From elementary school onward, we spend an inordinate amount of time focused on how we appear in the world. We carefully construct a narrative about ourselves, one usually masking our vulnerabilities. Our motivation, in part, stems from the fact we are trying to get people to like us, to be attracted to us. We wonder, *how can anyone like me if I let them see me without makeup, with bed hair, or in a foul mood?* So we hide.

True intimacy and connection (which deep down we crave) evolve through vulnerability. And we are most vulnerable when we are new to the world and on the precipice of exiting the world. As the caregivers of the young and the older, we are truly needed. Boundaries between people are erased.

Generally, these roles are not invited but thrust upon us and are often fraught with difficulty. There is the physical toll on our own bodies and the spiritual/emotional toll caused by our spending time away from our lives and interests. But juxtaposed with the hard stuff is the good stuff, the love, tenderness, and intimacy. We often dread the prospect of becoming a caregiver, but these experiences offer an opportunity to deepen our connection with our loved ones and recognize in ourselves our capacity for love and kindness.

It had been a long time since a little boy needed me so much (and for that matter, even a big one!) Just like the Grinch whose heart grew three times its size, I think my own heart grew a little too following my stint as a caregiver.

CREATIVE LIVING IS A PATH FOR THE BRAVE

On occasion, I take my creativity crusade on the road. I was invited to conduct workshops at The Myositis Association's annual conference in New Orleans. Myositis takes many forms—Lupus, Rheumatoid Arthritis, and severe muscle weakness, to name a few. The first session I conducted was designed for patients with autoimmune disorders; the second addressed issues facing caregivers of loved ones suffering from these debilitating diseases.

Even though I do not suffer from an autoimmune disorder, I wanted to convey my passionate belief that having an illness or caring for someone who does needn't doom one to a poor quality of life. Creativity is obviously not a panacea, but it is helpful. The 2015 documentary, *A Dose of Creativity*, enumerates the benefits of creative engagement among aging adults: fewer doctors' visits, fewer prescription drugs, memory enhancement, fewer falls, a sense of belonging, and "a second chance at life," according to one of the budding artists in the documentary.[2]

I came to the conference loaded with statistics and suggestions for creative coping techniques. As is often the case, though, I was the one walking away feeling enriched. I carried home stories about acute pain, muscle inflammation and weakness, negative reactions to medications, falls, even death. I listened to the stories of spouses describing their multiple roles and responsibilities and having little to no time left over for their own pursuits. A young husband became emotional, describing how he missed physical intimacy with his wife of only two years. I heard about the "toys" people purchased to help them function—motorized wheelchairs, bidets, vans with special lifts. But what I was most moved by was the obvious love and devotion between patient and caregiver. I heard a sweet story from one husband who said his own creativity had blossomed since the onset of his wife's illness. His wife was a quilter, and he had taken to cutting out fabric for her, as she could no longer squeeze a pair of scissors. They had become closer than even before her illness because of these shared activities.

I was struck by the bravery. It was brave that these attendees showed up to the conference. Bravery is mustering an inner strength you might not have realized was even a part of your makeup. Sure, bravery is required to climb a mountain or parachute from a plane. True bravery, however, is made up of little everyday heroics.

Remember *BBLB Manual of Maxims* #23: "Bravery is about saying yes, and . . . "

"Yes, my husband has a grave illness, *and* I'm going to be open and accepting about what this new phase offers."

I was honored and happy for the opportunity to meet real heroes that weekend.

CREATING PEACE WITH YOUR OWN TWO HANDS

Speaking of heroes, I had the privilege of conducting a two-part workshop entitled, "Creating Peace with Your Own Two Hands" for a group of caregivers. These pre-Covid sessions were held at a facility dedicated to strengthening the mind, body, and spirit. And the spirits of the participants I met seriously needed strengthening.

Everything about this center, from the architecture to the meditation gardens, promotes a sense of peace and wellbeing. It was the perfect venue for the healing we hoped would happen for people whose lives had been turned upside down by debilitating illnesses.

My two-part pottery session focused on plate glazing. Participants were invited to create six-word stories expressing their feelings. You might remember from one of our Exercise Your Creativity practices, Ernest Hemingway is credited with originating this form of flash fiction. The six-word stories composed by our budding writers mirrored the poignancy of Hemingway's "For sale, Baby shoes, Never worn." These stories were inscribed in glaze on dinner plates.

"Doing Your Best is Never Enough," a story composed by Daniel, reflected his despair over his care partner's frustrations. A more positive six-word story came from Lisa— "There Is Always a Silver Lining." Pat inscribed, "This Is Harder than I Thought," reflecting her reactions to the creative exercise and her caregiving journey.

CREATIVITY IS OBVIOUSLY NOT a panacea, but I believe it encourages mindfulness. As *Enrich Your Caregiving Journey* author, Margie Pabst-Steinmetz says,

> *As a caregiver, activities that use our hands also reduce stress as tensions melt into creations—green shoots breaking the soil, a clay cup fired from the kiln or a melody breaking the silence or noise of the day. When we use our hands to create, we discover solace and create peaceful moments for ourselves and our care partners.*[3]

As is often the case, I came to the workshop equipped with statistics and coping techniques, but I'm the one who walked away feeling enriched and humbled by the sagas shared. On our second day, a participant, her voice cracking, shared that her husband's death was imminent. As she raged against the ineptitude of the nursing home, her love and devotion was palpable. My fervent hope during our time together was that these caregivers experienced a respite, using their hands not just to create a piece of art but peace for their spirits.

THE ARTS AS A BEACON OF HOPE

The E.A. Michelson Philanthropy, formerly Aroha Philanthropies, champions programs that break barriers, build community, and spark creativity. The Philanthropy funds arts programs that empower older adults to discover their capabilities and form connections with others. While this initiative is targeted primarily to caregivers and those "age 55 and better," I see its application for caregivers and care partners of all ages. I know my mother cared for me and loved me, but I'm not sure she hoisted my emotional traumas on to her shoulders in the same way we do with our children. Or perhaps we just did not share them with our parents in the same way we have encouraged our children to share theirs with us.

My daughter underwent a very real trauma in her early thirties. While intellectually I know the experience was more difficult for her than for me, I don't know if it could have been that much greater considering the extent to which I felt her pain. (I know I know. My boundaries were nonexistent during this time.) Living in another state made access more difficult, so there were many telephone calls, FaceTime sessions, and a plane trip to Florida. And creativity was an integral part of our care exchange. One weekend during this difficult time, we filled a shopping cart at Michael's craft store with clay, buttons, paint, and canvases. Then we devoted an entire day to creating. It really didn't matter what we made; what mattered was that we took part in the process of creating. Hallmark holiday movies accompanied our sculpting and scrapbooking as my family room assumed the role of an art studio with bits of paper, polymer clay, and glitter strewn about. So, what!

Cleaning only took minutes. The process and products have lasted in our hearts ever since.

I STOLE MY HUSBAND (HIS FORMER WIFE PROBABLY THINKS THAT TOO)

As our parents crested toward their seventies, we weren't surprised when they began experiencing health issues requiring our attention. It was the natural order of things. That's what happens when people grow old. But I don't think we paused to consider the same fate for ourselves and our partners. At least I didn't until my then seventy-two-year-old fit as a fiddle husband had a cancer scare.

The dreaded C word you never want to hear. "Our scan shows a mass in your abdomen," pronounced the doctor at an urgent care center. My husband had been suffering with abdominal pain for several weeks. "You need to get a nuclear scan to determine if it's a carcinoid tumor."

In hindsight, we shouldn't have driven immediately to the emergency room, but we were desperate for more definitive information. We were hoping for a nuclear medicine scan or biopsy as quickly as possible. My husband's cancer scare occurred during the second year of the pandemic when access to medical care was inhibited by the influx of Covid cases.

We waited in the Advent Health Emergency Room for hours hoping for a bed to become available. The ER nurse compared our queuing experience with the long lines she witnessed during a visit to Russia as a high schooler. "People waited for hours to see a doctor. Now the same thing is happening here. We keep running out of medical supplies and people can't get the medical treatment they need we are so overwhelmed."

Meanwhile, abject fear became a constant companion. My dog does this thing where she comes up and leans into me for stroking and attention. I felt the same need, wanting to lean into my husband for comfort and assurance.

Once a hospital room finally became available my husband was held hostage for two days. Two days in which nothing happened. Hours passed between nurse or doctor visits. There was no radiologist available to perform a nuclear scan. I just wish they had mentioned that fact when we checked in to the ER.

On the second afternoon, I asked if my husband could go downstairs to enjoy the beautiful weather. "Sure, I'll let the charge nurse know," promptly replied the hospitalist, happy to mitigate his guilt for ordering the fourteen hour food fast in anticipation of the biopsy he was now aborting. "Let's blow this joint!" I whispered. "I'm taking you home." When I mentioned to a friend that I had kidnapped my husband from the hospital, she was horrified. "He had an IV in his forearm! What if you had gotten into an accident?!"

Our home is less than ten minutes from the hospital, and I'm a safe driver. I carefully situated Jim in our Subaru (one of the safest cars on the highway) and brought him to the comfort of his recliner. We felt giddy with freedom. I prepared a healthy meal to break his fast and returned him two hours later to his hospital room. Apparently, no one had even noticed his absence; his room was in the same state as when we left. But that little act of rebellion gave us a sense of power and control in a situation where we felt powerless.

While BBLB advocates breaking a few pesky rules, it doesn't encourage reckless disregard for medical or organizational policies and procedures. I wanted to keep my husband away from other hospital patients and visitors who might be contagious, and those two hours in his own home, nuzzling with his labradoodle, helped soothe his fears and lift his spirit. It was totally worth it!

BBLB Manual of Maxims #33:
"Take calculated risks."

Rules provide scaffolding for society. Institutions, like medical facilities, require them to keep people and employees safe. I'm grateful for protocols designed to protect patients. But some of the fine print rules beg to be broken. I also draw a distinction between protocols and obsequious etiquette. Medical personnel bow down and seemingly pay homage to doctors. Now, I like most doctors. Two of my dearest friends who helped me navigate our cancer scare are doctors. But the colorectal surgeon who removed the tumor from Jim's abdomen during his second hospitalization behaved more like Napoleon than someone who took the Hippocratic oath to do no harm. And when we saw him, he was never without his entourage of young, beautiful interns. "The surgery was more complicated than I expected," he said without any evidence of compassion. "There were multiple growths. The pathology report should be back in seven to ten days. I inserted a nasogastric (NG) tube down his nose into his stomach." And then he left the surgical waiting room and me with my mouth agape.

"I need Xanax," I pleaded in my 911 call to my friend, Ann.

My husband was a mess. He choked and gagged on the nasal tube for two excruciatingly long days. I begged nurses to contact the doctor. A STAT x-ray was performed to determine the placement of the tube. It had never made it down to the stomach but was tangled in his esophagus. The floor doctor finally ordered its removal. The surgeon did not appear until the following day. I resorted to buying gift cards for the nursing staff, hoping the bribe would keep some of their focus on room 321.

It was an awful experience. Access to medical care during the time of Covid was a nightmare. Our emotions teeter-tottered between euphoria at good news and despondency at scary news. And then there were the visits from Anxiety, waking me up every morning at 4:30 murmuring her morose messages.

I do believe in the concept of God. For some reason, however, my lips refused to utter prayerful words. But other people did. There were prayer chains from Southern Illinois to Winter Park, Florida. I question whether outside prayer works. But just knowing they were praying was as comforting as a warm bath. God truly manifested herself through the love and kindness of friends. Cards, cappuccinos, even cough drops were dropped off, as were meals and bushels of fruit. We felt lifted up and cared for.

There is a caveat to all the caring, however. I got overwhelmed by texts, phone calls, and offers of food. Then one morning, my daughter gave me good advice. "Mom," she said, "you don't have to be so polite." There was something sublimely simple about that counsel. I've spent my entire life being a pleaser. To me, good manners are a must. But Tracy was right. I didn't have the emotional bandwidth to be gracious, and I didn't have to respond to every text or call. Accepting that fact gave me back some of the strength that kept threatening to evaporate.

WHAT EXACTLY IS EMOTIONAL DEPENDENCY?

The whole health care experience made me ponder the term "dependency." Lady Boomers probably prolonged our children's adolescence by enabling their dependence on us. I spent the better part of a chapter bemoaning this truth and how our enabling patterns postponed many of our own passions and dreams. But maybe it works both ways. During my husband's medical crisis, my kids were rocks, allowing me to collapse like a deflated balloon. All those years of validating their feelings was reciprocated. Their calls, presents, and presence eased stress. They even introduced me to Wordle, a game we played together online.

I also realized the interdependency between my husband and me. Our partnership has been one aspect of our relationship we value the most, but I don't think I quite realized how much Jim does to make our lives function. Suddenly, I was the one making sure the trash and recycling was taken to the curb on the right days. I was the one walking the dog twice a day. Our aging labradoodle decided her failing hips wouldn't allow her to climb our stairs any longer. So rather than my strong husband giving her a boost, that job fell to my back. All those little everyday tasks became mine.

The other interdependency issue I observed was my propensity to use collective words like "our," "us," and "we."

"*Our* hospital room is on the third floor."

"*We* are going to the doctor on Tuesday."

"Thank you for caring about *us*."

My husband's plight became mine too. I didn't know where he ended and I began. But is this necessarily the negative I anticipated? The daily showering and bandaging fostered intense intimacy between us. And, as I've proposed earlier in this book, maybe establishing intimacy is one of the great truths of life. When we love someone, we expose ourselves to vulnerability. And vulnerability is scary! Our intimacy extended to the mutual joy we experienced upon receiving the encouraging results from the pathology report.

BBLB Manual of Maxims #34:
"Allowing yourself to be vulnerable is brave."

Like most hospital visitors, I spent an inordinate amount of time waiting. Once again, however, creativity came to the rescue. A quilt I'd been working on since the onset of Covid provided much-needed focus for my mind and hands. The repetitive motion of hand stitching the binding to the quilt backing was calming. I took the advice cited earlier in this chapter "... when we use our hands to create, we discover solace and create peaceful moments for ourselves and our care partners."

GRAY IS THE NEW COLOR OF GRAFFITI

I'm addicted to alliteration—that literary device stringing words together that share a similar sound such as, "Sally sells seashells by the seashore . . ."

A SEGMENT FEATURED IN A 2016 NBC Nightly News broadcast was entitled, "Granny Does Graffiti." The alliterative title got me from the get-go. Mary Good, the painter and grandmother who was the subject of the segment, had been diagnosed with Alzheimer's disease. Mary attended a creative arts program designed for people with memory loss issues at an adult day care center in Denver, Colorado. Through art, the sadness she experienced at the erosion of her memory was temporarily erased through her engagement with the creative arts.[4]

But this program took creative expression to a new level. Mary's paintbrush had been replaced by a can of spray paint. Her new canvas, a wall. Demographically, these seniors don't fit the profile of graffiti artists, but the hope is that by introducing a novel kind of medium, different channels open up in the brain and it is possible to get a glimpse of the person who still lives there. Talk about novel! Graffiti art is often deemed an illegal violation of public spaces. How thrilling and a little daring for these older artists, even if their canvases happened to be sanctioned.

And Denver is not the only city promoting grandparent graffiti movements. Lisbon, Portugal created Lata 65 (Lata is "tin can" in Portuguese; 65 the historical age designation for senior citizens.) Sixty-five-year-olds are paired with street artists in workshops to learn the logistics of stencil making and spraying. The project is revitalizing and coloring the city with fresh perspectives from older sources.

To say I love these projects would be an understatement. Creative expression enriches lives. Why shouldn't it enrich our aging? According to their website, Lata 65 is creating "bad ass senior citizens who can find something in common with teenagers". Lata also means nerve. It takes nerve for older people to step outside their comfort zone and try something entirely new, and using graffiti art to reach people with memory issues is cool. A characteristic of our baby boomer generation is our quest to be cool. I think being budding Banksys, the street artist with an international reputation for cool, would totally fulfill that goal.

For many people, making art can be nerve-wracking. What am I going to make? What materials should I use? What if it . . . sucks? Studies show that despite those fears, engaging in any sort of artistic expression results in the reward pathway in the brain being activated, and, at least for a time, we feel good. It's easy to give up hope amid the grueling responsibilities of caregiving. Art helps us imagine a more hopeful future.

BBLB RECAP

The idea of striving for a perfect state of wellness for ourselves and our partners will only pitch us into a state of chronic dissatisfaction. Our goal should be acceptance of whatever state our mind and body occupy in the present moment.

BBLB Manual of Maxims # 35:
"Acceptance is an active state, not a passive one."

As author and philosopher, William B. Irvine said in his 2019 book, *The Stoic Challenge,* "There are going to be negative things that happen to you. Most of the damage done to you by things is not the event itself, but your reactions to it."[5]

As the ancient Stoic Philosophers taught, *do what you can with what you've got, where you are.*

Caregiving roles are generally not invited but thrust upon us. But juxtaposed with the hard stuff (exhaustion, stress, financial woes) is the good stuff (the love, tenderness, and intimacy). Part of what makes us human is our need for intimacy. This is your opportunity, not just your burden.

Creativity once again rides up to help the cause. Creative endeavors promote a sense of belonging and enhance mental and physical capabilities. You don't have to be a graffiti artist to be creative. Any hobby or passion will do.

And breaking a few fine print rules is justified. They are called "calculated risks." Minor acts of rebellion give you and your care partner a sense of control.

It takes bravery to refuse to settle for a diminished life as a caregiver or care partner. Bravery is about saying, "yes, and . . ." This isn't the first time we've had to put on our big girl pants. So, put them on and move forward.

My husband and I went to a favorite restaurant to celebrate his good pathology report. There were open seats at the bar, so we ordered cocktails. My husband's Manhattan was accompanied by a large ice cube designed to slowly release the flavors of the bourbon. It was fun. We ordered appetizers. We talked and flirted. He was my husband again, not my patient. Striving for a good quality of life should be a lifelong pursuit.

EXERCISE YOUR CREATIVITY #9:

CREATE YOUR OWN PERSONAL TALISMAN

A talisman is thought to have magical powers and is said to connect the one who possesses it to the spiritual world. You may be more familiar with an amulet, which is typically a small piece of jewelry thought to give protection against evil, danger, and disease. The person who plans to use a talisman should be the one to create it. During medieval times, medical practitioners often prescribed talisman for divine protection and even for specific medical issues like conceiving a child. While conception may not be uppermost in our minds, a dose of protection, especially amid Covid's aftermath, might be very welcome.

Since you will be the person creating your talisman, you can choose any medium. Clay, metal, stones, fabric, gems, mosaic tiles, or beads are perfect for creating. A talisman often includes geometric designs, astrological symbols, even pentagrams. It can incorporate a favorite poem, religious verse, or even your six-word story. Pinterest and Etsy sites have many examples of talismans and amulets for your reference. Remember, in the BBLB world, there are no rules for this exercise. This is by and for you.

Whether talismans are magical or not, we need an object reminding us to keep the faith. The act of creating connects us with the divine.

CHAPTER 10:

What's Next, Boomer?

*"The greatest potential for growth and self-realization
exists in the second half of life."*
—CARL JUNG

Being brave, exercising your sass, rebelling against a few pesky fine print rules, and being the boss of your hours and minutes are themes I've sought to convey in this book. *Be Brave, Lose the Beige!* is a philosophy, a way of perceiving your world. Fundamental to this philosophy is creativity. Creative thinking is an excellent co-conspirator in the struggle to regain even a little control as we navigate our aging journeys. Henceforth, these years will be designated our BBLB years.

While creativity is fun, it's not made of magic. Snapping your fingers to summon creativity is not really a thing. There is a formula for developing your creative thinking skills. (And remember, it's never too late to start.) First, you must recognize the value of creative thinking. Next, you must do the work by exercising your creative muscles, many of which have threatened to atrophy in the years since you were ten. Hopefully, you have engaged in a few of *BBLB*'s *Exercise Your Creativity* prescriptions designed to prime your creative pumps. And third, you must be open and curious about the messages or intuitive sparks your creative brain whispers to you.

How did we lose our aptitude for coloring outside the lines? When did we start painting our goals, choices, and strategies beige? Why did we postpone our passions and wishes? By being the slice of boloney sandwiched between two demanding generations. We strived to fulfill the expectations and dreams of our mothers while simultaneously parenting our adult children. This juxtaposition managed to mute many of our Magenta impulses. We began our tenure as moms in a pickle because our mother figures established a standard for how to behave as moms while simultaneously projecting their own thwarted ambitions upon us. The outcome? A lot of guilt as we struggled to balance work life with child rearing. From the get-go, guilt robbed us of our jewel tones.

And when in the hell did we get so old? Why can't I read a restaurant menu without my iPhone flashlight? Why is every pair of pants I own black? When did I start wearing shoes that are good for my feet? These transitions can make us cranky. Inevitably, we will face health transitions, marital and sexual transitions, fashion transitions, even restaurant transitions. How we occupy the space of these transitions determines whether our lives will be enriched or diminished by them.

Fear often causes us to erect barriers to ward off change. Rather than dreading or fretting about these changes, why not handle them as Peter Beagle suggested? Try walking through a few walls. Our lives have been bricked up with seconds and minutes, happy hours, and birthdates. Time is our God, and we are its flock of submissive followers. How we choose to navigate these passages makes us the boss of our BBLB minutes and hours.

If we ornery oldsters don't want to feel the pain inflicted by these life transitions, what do we do? First, we whip out our 1960s protest buttons and say no to the beige rules and expectations associated with aging. Second, we turn to the BBLB Rx pad. Just like medication for diabetes, BBLB prescriptions can help with aging ailments: Hold your friends dear, mindfulness is a must, find the silver linings, and choose to infuse even the most boring and monotonous tasks with color and fun. The potency (intensity) and dosage (frequency) of these prescriptions are up to you. Beware, however, these therapies can be addictive.

Absent from the list on the Rx pad are a few more homeopathic remedies not typically found on a doctor's prescription pad. More than a closeted few sixty-plus-year-olds have been turning to marijuana as a coping mechanism and to treat ailments associated with aging. Talk about a lightness of spirit! Perhaps this prescription will help you not care so much about the changes. And after a nest filled with human relatives, the buoyancy of our furry friends provides balm for tired spirits. They can also fill the intimacy gap. Nothing says intimacy like shoving your hand down the mouth of your golden retriever to retrieve the sock he's threatening to swallow. And the third postponed prescription? Dump that toxic relationship no matter what your age. Consider how much freer you might feel unencumbered by a controlling partner.

HOW DO WE AFFORD THESE therapies and other expenses required to get us through our BBLB years? Our retirement purses are not likely to resemble our parents' purses. We may face our golden years sans the gold. But perhaps we don't have to restrict our BBLB years to just one color. Let's put an innovative spin on baby boomer retirement options. Maybe even consider entrepreneurship. Self-employment makes sense because it allows for more control over working hours and conditions. Try taking your retirement a little at a time or even take a gap year as a trial run at retirement scenarios. Maybe communal living is an option for you. And just maybe, despite what financial planners have advised, we don't need as much gold as we thought we needed. The pandemic convinced me that downsizing our pocketbook spending does not mean downsizing our authentic quality of life.

Lady Boomers have a history of sharing their purses with loved ones. Are you such an angel? Do you step forward to assume emotional and financial responsibility for others? Such angels don't sprout wings or have halos. Even the self-sufficient among us, if given half an opportunity, will readily dive into the angel's amniotic fluid, languishing in their warm, nurturing, healing presence. But angels, if abused, can become reluctant and recalcitrant. Assuming others' financial woes and anxieties can overburden them, causing them to cash in their angel careers or morph into martyrs. The world needs the angels among us. So, before maxing out, try establishing a few boundaries, and invest in relationships that are two-sided. It's not worth the calorie burn to exist in a one-sided relationship. Establishing boundaries is tough. It's like trying to train a dog; hard to be consistent, but worth the effort to have a non-barking, non-jumping canine.

The danger of becoming a reluctant angel extends to our caregiving roles as well. Establishing boundaries is even more important in this capacity. Being a caregiver for the young or the old can be taxing. But don't despair, juxtaposed with the hard stuff—exhaustion, stress, financial woes—is the good stuff, the love, tenderness, and intimacy. And part of what makes us human is our need for intimacy. Caregiving responsibilities can be perceived as an opportunity for intimacy rather than just a burden.

Our goal for ourselves and care partners can be to accept our current state of mental and physical wellness. Striving for a perfect state of wellness for ourselves and our partners will only pitch us into a state of chronic dissatisfaction. As recommended by the ancient Stoic philosophers, do what you can with what you've got, where you are. Thinking creatively about this phase in our lives will help inform our attitudes. Remember BBLB Manual of Maxims #35: "Acceptance is an active state, not a passive one."

What is our reward for all the caregiving we've administered throughout our years? Of course, serving loved ones is a reward in itself. But the ultimate reward? Grandparenting. Being a grandparent is like eating an ice cream sundae every day, with no calorie penalties. It's delicious. It's our reward for having kids. But how do we manage the juxtaposition of our physical changes with enjoying our sought-after grandparenting gig? You rock the look, that's how. You behave in such a way that your biological or foster grandchildren will believe every one of your lines and wrinkles is beautiful. Following the GRP (Grand-mother's Rules of Procedure) guidelines can help achieve that goal: Shine a light for your children. Remind them most spats and injuries are temporary; be useful, helping when you can; be indulgent and skirt a few pesky parental rules; avoid playing the victim card; keep your mouth shut; and don't sacrifice yourself. Pain and exhaustion have the potential to zap your sass.

As an avowed creativity evangelist, I began this book preaching the importance and benefits of creative thinking. I thought I knew what it meant to be brave and poke fun at certain societal rules and expectations. That is, until I wrote this book. I underestimated how owning these qualities in myself might evolve. *Be Brave. Lose the Beige! Finding Your Sass After Sixty* started out on a linear path. But it dipped and curved, and I felt my writing grow braver with each chapter revision. By sharing my formulas, I learned them too. Starting out, I did not imagine that by chapter six, I would entitle one of my subchapters, "Purses are Like Vaginas." I got bolder in my language. As a blogger, I hesitated to use the "F" word for fear of offending someone. The process of writing this book eased that inhibition.

I was working on my "Caregivers Living in Color" chapter during my husband's 2022 cancer surgery. "You don't have to be so polite, mom," counseled my daughter one day when I was overwhelmed by texts and phone calls with offers of help. I wove that advice into my chapter revisions. I realized I have a pathological propensity to please others, and I don't think I'm alone. I know many other Lady Boomers who suffer from their own approval addictions. Did society and our parents subtly and not so subtly encourage us to adopt these roles? Or is it in our DNA to be sensitive and caring? Either way, it is incumbent upon us to get braver and set boundaries to protect ourselves and stop postponing our own lives.

You don't have to be perfect in the execution of the steps and prescriptions offered in this book. Far from it. Striving for perfection is another one of those boomer behaviors that erode our color and zap our sass. Just be open and try a couple. The responses will reward your efforts.

WHAT'S NEXT FOR LADY BOOMERS?

I'm already seeing it. I know women in their sixties, seventies, and eighties who have broken up with body parts or lost partners. The loss has been wrenching. But, like trampled flowers, I see them rising back up. Women create pods with like-situated women. They sit together during religious services, attend cultural events together, and travel, sharing VRBO rentals or cruise cabins. I'm awed by the resilience. Women carry on. They adapt and create other forms of community. Maybe I'm not just proud to be a baby boomer, I'm proud to be a Lady Boomer. We don't quit in the face of hardships. We carry on and make meaning.

I turned seventy as this book was being published. Would the title remain relevant if I was aging into my seventies, I fretted. Would I live to enjoy its publication? These were questions and anxieties plaguing me as Brother Time sought to steal more of my minutes and hours. I suspect you might have similar questions about your futures. However, your creative brains will probably say, "Yes! Go for it." Whether we are entering our sixties or nineties, the messages still apply. We are women who are entering what may be the last third of our lives. If we aren't brave and sassy now, when will we ever be?

My editor asked me to write a bio for book promotion purposes. It ended up being several paragraphs long because I did not know what to leave out or include. Lady Boomers have worn a lot of hats during our lifetimes: Blogger, second wife, mom, fun grandmother, potter, enabling dog owner, curious researcher, program founder, bike rider. If you look behind you, your list will be quite long. So, this is my next-to-last assignment for you. Write your own bio. Leave nothing out. Brag and bemoan. It will be surprisingly enlightening.

EXERCISE YOUR CREATIVITY #10:

TAKE THE KQUIZ

As I've reported, my husband and I have been in the market research business for over thirty years. As we considered what our own futures might look like, we created a survey/quiz to help us and others gain insight into their values, personality traits, and motivations as we stand at the juncture of retirement or semi-retirement.

The KQuiz was designed with the sixty-plus age demographic in mind. Most of us have taken at least one personality test in our lives. The question is, do the profiles we were given hold up as we age into our sixties, seventies, eighties, and beyond? Find out where your partner is on these dimensions and determine where you intersect and differ. The results will provide you with a pretty good road map going forward.

The KQuiz is based upon archetypes. Carl Jung, the founder of analytic psychology, identified archetypes that symbolize basic human motivations. Each type has its own set of values, meanings, and personality traits, and most people have more than one archetype at play in their personalities. Generally, however, one archetype tends to dominate. It's helpful to know which archetypes are at play in you and your loved ones to gain personal insight into behaviors and motivations.

Are you a Sage, the visionary?
Are you the Dreamer who strives for authenticity?
Are you the Rebel, the spontaneous non-conformist?
Are you the Caretaker, the conscientious one?

Type the following URL http://www.whatsnextboomer .com into your internet browser to take the quiz. It's never too late to learn more about yourself. The following is an example of how each of the archetypes might handle the winter holidays. Find yourself in these descriptions:

THE REBEL

Arguably, the Rebel may have the most fun of all the archetypes during the winter holidays. Rebels by their natures are fun loving, and what could be more fun than this colorful, musically imbued holiday season? They are more likely to embellish their homes with colorful lights and decorations, perhaps verging on the garish side (they believe in keeping the GAWD in Christmas.) Now, don't expect your Rebel to have actually prepared for the holidays. They truly fall into the last-minute shoppers' category. The "hot" new toys may well be sold out by the time the Rebel gets around to shopping. They are the proverbial kids on Christmas morning and will be on the floor or in the driveway playing with grandchildren and their new toys and games. Rebels also make entertaining holiday dinner guests. They add lively conversation and jokes at the dinner table, just don't expect them to arrive on time. Rebels are not big on tradition and may like to vary their holiday experiences, perhaps traveling one year, hosting the next, or visiting friends and relatives the year after.

THE DREAMER

All are welcome to share in the Dreamer's holiday

festivities. "Leave no one behind" might well be the Dreamer's mantra. They can't bear to think about anyone spending the holidays alone (even if that person really would just like to enjoy a little downtime.) "Mothering" is the Dreamer's MO. They can't resist clucking, nurturing, and including. Dreamers will also enjoy the creative component of the holidays decorating with a flourish—and rest assured their decorations will be unique, like the one-of-a-kind handmade ceramic nativity scene or Menorah. A gift from the Dreamer will invariably be thoughtful, reflecting their insight into the personality of the recipient. They also may give altruistic presents—contributions to a favorite charity or environmental organization. When or where to celebrate the holidays is less important to the Dreamer than being with children and grandchildren. Dreamers love spending time with their families.

THE SAGE

The Sage is likely to enjoy the cultural aspects of the season. Handel's *Messiah*, *The Nutcracker*, or a production of *A Christmas Carol* is right up the Sage's alley. In retirement, the Sage might become a member of a choral group or orchestra and perform holiday music. Gifts given by the Sage may be educational—books, gifts from travel destinations, or even a subscription to *National Geographic*. The Sage may not like all the fuss and muss of the holidays, preferring simpler, more minimalistic decorations. The Sage might be willing to forego decorations altogether and use the holiday ➤

➤ break as a time for travel to an interesting destination. Even in retirement, the Sage is unlikely to just sit around during the holidays, preferring instead to look for intellectually challenging things to do. While not terribly social, the Sage will still enjoy discussing world events with interesting family members or teaching grandchildren how to use newly acquired telescopes or toys. The Sage will actually read the "some assembly required" instructions.

THE CARETAKER

Caretakers value maintaining family traditions passed down from year to year. Whether it's attending midnight services on Christmas Eve or lighting candles each night during Chanukah, the Caretaker tends to honor family customs. The Caretaker is the best prepared of all the archetypes for the holidays, shopping and buying gifts throughout the year, mindful of sales, which help them stay within budget. You won't find the Caretaker in a frenzy buying last-minute presents or hastily assembling decorations two days before Christmas. Speaking of decorations, the Caretaker's house is more likely to be tastefully decorated using white lights and traditional mangers or menorahs. From a gift-giving standpoint, Caretakers probably lean toward the practical side, giving useful presents that can be used throughout the year.

I hope this quiz helps you find what's next for you.

My ADD brain takes a circuitous route, and, if this book has taught me anything, that is the very definition of creativity. So for all of you who have felt marginalized or left out because your brain tends not to function along linear lines, this book is for you. I hope it can be your companion and cheerleader, encouraging you to say yes to yourself and gently break free of some of those pesky fine print rules.

The BBLB Manual of Maxims

#1   Exercise your creative muscles.

#2   It's easier to ask for forgiveness than permission.

#3   Breaking little rules is empowering.

#4   Don't be afraid to break with convention.
     It's liberating and might inspire others.

#5   Be brave and open to changes and life transitions.

#6   Don't be a victim.

#7   Cultivate a sense of humor.

#8   Parenting is not a popularity contest.

#9   Yes, your children's shit really does stink.

#10 Don't let kid demands derail the pursuit of
     your passions.

#11 Don't let time be your boss.

#12 Hold your friends dear.

#13 Be kind and patient with yourself during major changes.

#14 Allow comfort to govern your fashion choices.

#15 Don't be an entitled old person.

#16 Don't worship at the feet of Brother Time.
     Pay homage to Sister Space.

#17 Seek out the silver linings.

#18 Be brave. Don't accept physical limitations.
     Invent your own definition of athleticism.

#19   Try wasting a day.

#20   Don't neglect romance. Touch is as important in our BBLB years as it ever was.

#21   Got gummies?

#22   Try some pet therapy.

#23   Bravery is about saying Yes, and . . .

#24   If need be, dump the dude.

#25   Accepting the state of our purses equals accepting ourselves.

#26   Stay foolish.

#27   Live in community with one another.

#28   Your purse doesn't have to match your clothes.

#29   Avoid becoming someone's oxygen tank.

#30   Let's serve as God's proxies.

#31   Following the GRP guidelines will sass up your role as grandmother.

#32   Instead of playing the guilt card, play the reframing card. It's transformative.

#33   Take calculated risks.

#34   Allowing yourself to be vulnerable is brave.

#35   Acceptance is an active state, not a passive one.

Notes

CHAPTER 1

1. Laura Holson, "We're All Artists Now," *New York Times*, September 4, 2015, https://www.nytimes.com /2015/09/06/opinion/were-all-artists-now.html.
2. "Is Creating Art Good for the Aging Brain?," *Better Aging*, December 4, 2019, https://www.betteraging .com/cognitive-aging/art-aging-brain/.
3. Elizabeth Gilbert, *Big Magic: Creative Living Beyond Fear*, (New York: Penguin Publishing Group, 2016).
4. "Participating in the Arts Creates Paths to Healthy Aging", *National Institute of Health, US Department of Health and Human Services*, February 15, 2019, https://www.nia.nih.gov/news/participating -arts-creates-paths-healthy-aging
5. Daniela Pavan, "Can We Train Our Creative Muscles?," *Forbes*, May 10, 2019, https://www.forbes.com/sites /forbesagencycouncil/2019/05/10/can-we-train-our -creative-muscles/?sh=676279c62c8d.
6. Jeffrey Kluger, "How to Live Long," *Time Magazine*, September 23, 2019, https://time.com/625/how-to -live-long/.

7. M.C. Richards, *Centering: In Pottery, Poetry, and the Person*, (Middletown: Wesleyan University Press, 1989).

8. Sunni Brown, *The Doodle Revolution: Unlock the Power to Think Differently*, (New York: The Penguin Group, 2015).

CHAPTER 2

1. Betty Friedan, *The Feminine Mystique*, (New York: W.W. Norton, 1963).

2. Maria, "Top 10 Most Popular Sports in America in 2022," *SVSports Virsa*, January 3, 2020, https://sports virsa.com/most-popular-sports-in-america/.

3. Elizabeth Yuko, "Out of sorts Around the Holidays? It Could be Family Jet Lag," *The New York Times*, December 22, 2016, https://www.nytimes.com/2016 /12/22/well/family/out-of-sorts-around-the-holidays -it-could-be-family-jet-lag.html.

CHAPTER 3

1. Michele Willens, "When Did We Get So Old?," *New York Times*, August 30, 2014, https://www.nytimes .com/2014/08/31/sunday-review/the-boomers-biggest -challenge.html.

2. Frank Bruni, "The Best Restaurant If You're Over 50," *New York Times*, March 30, 2019, https://www .nytimes.com/2019/03/30/opinion/sunday/best- restaurant-over-50.html.

3. "Retired Husband Syndrome", *ABC News/GMA*, January 11, 2006, https://abcnews.go.com/GMA /AmericanFamily/story?id=1491039

4. Tim Gunn, "The Fashion Industry is not Making it Work for Plus-sized Women," *NPR*, September 14, 2016, https://www.npr.org/2016/09/14/493965878/tim -gunn-the-fashion-industry-is-not-making-it-work -for-plus-size-women.
5. Elizabeth Yuko, "A Letter From the Contents of My Bra Drawer," *New York Times,* April 28, 2020, https://www.nytimes.com/2020/04/28/style/bras-at -home-coronavirus.html.
6. José Andrés, *We Fed an Island: The True Story of Re-Building Puerto Rico, One Meal at a Time,* (New York: Harper Collins, 2018).

CHAPTER 4

1. Lisa Feldman Barrett, "How to Become a 'Superager'," *New York Times*, December 31, 2016, https://www .nytimes.com/2016/12/31/opinion/sunday/how-to -become-a-superager.html.
2. "Evaluating the Evidence on Sitting, Smoking, and Health. Is Sitting the New Smoking?" *AJPH, American Journal of Public Health,* November, 2018, https ://ajph.aphapublications.org/doi/10.2105/AJPH.2018 .304649
3. Patricia Hampl, *The Art of the Wasted Day,* (New York: Penguin Books, 2019)
4. Paige Bierma and Chris Woolston, "Sex and Aging," *HealthDay.* June 13, 2021, https://consumer.healthday .com/encyclopedia/aging-1/age-health-news-7/sex -and-aging-647539.html.

CHAPTER 5

1. Christopher Ingraham, "Aging baby boomers Increasingly embrace marijuana, heavier alcohol use," *The Washington Post,* December 18, 2016, https://www.washingtonpost.com/news/wonk/wp/2016/12/18/aging-boomers-increasingly-embrace-marijuana-heavy-alcohol-use/.

2. Tamara Holmes, "Baby Boomers Helping to Fuel Pet Market", *Yahoo Finance,* December 6, 2019, https://www.yahoo.com/video/baby-boomers-helping-fuel-pet-153954968.html

CHAPTER 6

1. Catherine Collinson, (2019, December), "19th Annual Transamerica Retirement Survey," *Transamerica Center for Retirement Studies,* 2019, https://transamericacenter.org/retirement-research/19th-annual-retirement-survey.

2. Lorie Konish, "Women are more likely to leave financial planning to their spouses. Here's why that's a problem," *CNBC,* March 18, 2019, https://www.cnbc.com/2019/03/18/women-are-more-likely-to-leave-money-decisions-to-their-spouses.html.

3. Laurent Belsie, "Why the Pandemic Forced Baby Boomers to Re-think Retirement Plans," *Christian Science Monitor,* June 1, 2021, https://www.csmonitor.com/Business/2021/0601/Why-pandemic-forced-baby-boomers-to-rethink-retirement-plans.

4. "Connecting to reimagine: Money & COVID-19," GFLEC, The Global Financial Literacy ExcellencCenter, 20220, https://gflec.org/webinar-videos/.

5. Peggy Klaus, "Embrace Your Age, and Conquer the World," *New York Times,* September 14, 2013,

https://www.nytimes.com/2013/09/15/jobs/embrace
-your-age-and-conquer-the-world.html.

6. Bejamin F. Jones, "Age and Great Invention," Kellogg Insight, Kellogg School of Management at Northwestern University, May 19, 2011, https://insight.kellogg .northwestern.edu/article/age_and_great_invention.

7. Steve Jobs, "You've Got to Find What You Love!" *Stanford News* June 14, 2005

8. Mark Miller, "You Don't Have to be College-Bound to Take a Gap Year," *New York Times,* July 14, 2017, https://www.nytimes.com/2017/07/14/your-money /you-dont-have-to-be-college-bound-to-take-a-gap -year.html.

9. Taylor Lorenz, "'OK Boomer' Marks the End of Friendly Generational Relations," *The New York Times,* January 15, 2020, https://www.nytimes.com/2019/10 /29/style/ok-boomer.html.

CHAPTER 7

1. Clare Ansberry, "Baby Boomers Get More Selective about Friends," *The Wall Street Journal,* July 18, 2018, https://www.wsj.com/articles/baby-boomers-get -more-selective-about-friends-1531918772.

CHAPTER 8

1. Lesley Stahl, "Boomer Grandparents Play Mom and Dad Part-Time," *CBS News,* April 3, 2016, https://www .cbsnews.com/video/boomer-grandparents-play -mom-and-dad-part-time/.

CHAPTER 9

1. Suleika Jaouad, *Between Two Kingdoms: A Memoir of a Life Interrupted*, (New York: Random House, 2021).
2. Aroha Philanthropies, "A Dose of Creativity," YouTube, November 6, 2015, https://www.youtube.com/watch?v=ERTfSz_8uZM.
3. Margery Pabst, *Enrich Your Caregiving Journey*, (Andover: Expert Publishing, Inc., 2009).
4. "Granny Does Graffiti," *NBC Nightly News*, October 10, 2016, https://www.youtube.com/watch?v=vwhs5cQ6RXg.
5. William Irvine, *The Stoic Challenge: A Philosopher's Guide to Becoming Tougher, Calmer, and More Resilient*, (New York: W.W. Norton & Co., 2019).

Acknowledgments

N o author puts a book out into the world alone. While
this isn't a cookbook, creating this book required a
number of ingredients: A measure of inspiration, a good
teacher, a whole lot of love and support, and a dash of skill.

I want to acknowledge my faithful *Be Brave. Lose
the Beige!* blog subscribers, many of whom have been
with me since 2009 at its onset. Their comments and kind
words have made me realize I'm not writing in the dark
and that my words can help. My blog posts formed the
nucleus of this book project.

I want to thank my husband, children, grandchildren,
and friends for actively or inadvertently supplying my pen
with inspiration for my stories. I hope my candor does
not offend. The point of writing this book was to help
people realize they are not alone. We are one through our
shared experiences.

I want to thank Brooke Warner, my publisher and
writing guru. I discovered Brooke through her Write-
minded podcast and was drawn to her writing wisdom
and publishing expertise. I'm proud to be a member of
the She Writes Press family. Thank you to Jodi Fodor, my
editor at She Writes Press. All the revisions and rewrites

she required of me made my writing clearer and richer. Between Brooke and Jodi, I feel like I've just finished my dissertation for a PhD.

And, as macabre as it may sound, I must acknowledge the impact of the pandemic on this writing project. Since we had nowhere to go and nowhere to be, I had no excuse but to use the time gifted me by this metaphorical comma and write, revise, and rewrite.

And I'm utterly and completely grateful to you, dear reader, for deeming this book worthy of your time and attention.

Thank you,
Liz Kitchens

About the Author

LIZ KITCHENS is a rare and endangered species born and raised in Orlando, Florida. Her memories of the sweet scent of orange blossoms and of the salty scrubbiness of the landscape pre-dates Walt Disney World. This geographical legacy, sandwiched between the frolicking waters of the Atlantic Ocean and Gulf Coast, inspired her playful spirit and informs her writing. She conducts workshops and seminars on creativity and directed a creative arts program for teens in underserved communities. She has also been a market researcher for thirty-five years and is the founder of *What's Next Boomer?* a website dedicated to helping boomers navigate retirement options; and of the blog, *Be Brave. Lose the Beige,* which focuses on issues facing women of the baby boomer generation. She is a contributing writer for the online magazine, *Sixty and Me,* and has been published in various online and print publications. Liz is married, the mother of three adult children, and the grandmother of three grandchildren.

Author photo © https://www.headshotorlando.com/

SELECTED TITLES FROM SHE WRITES PRESS

She Writes Press is an independent publishing company founded to serve women writers everywhere. Visit us at www.shewritespress.com.

Flip-Flops After Fifty: And Other Thoughts on Aging I Remembered to Write Down by Cindy Eastman. $16.95, 978-1-93831-468-1. A collection of frank and funny essays about turning fifty—and all the emotional ups and downs that come with it.

A Delightful Little Book on Aging by Stephanie Raffelock. $19.95, 978-1-63152-840-8. A collection of thoughts and stories woven together with a fresh philosophy that helps to dispel some of the toxic stereotypes of aging, this inspirational, empowering, and emotionally honest look at life's journey is part joyful celebration and part invitation to readers to live life fully to the very end.

No Spring Chicken: Stories and Advice from a Wild Handicapper on Aging and Disability by Francine Falk-Allen. $16.95, 978-1-64742-120-5. A companion to Falk-Allen's memoir *Not a Poster Child*, this handbook deftly and humorously shares tips and stories about disability-oriented travel, how to "be with" and adapt to a handicapped or aging person, and simple assistive health care we can employ in order to live our best and longest lives.

Notes from the Bottom of the World by Suzanne Adam. $16.95, 978-1-63152-415-8. In this heartfelt collection of sixty-three personal essays, Adam considers how her American past and move to Chile have shaped her life and enriched her worldview, and explores with insight questions on aging, women's roles, spiritual life, friendship, love, and writers who inspire.

The Book of Old Ladies: Celebrating Women of a Certain Age in Fiction by Ruth O. Saxton. $16.95, 978-1-63152-797-5. In this book lover's guide to approaching old age and its losses while still embracing beauty, sensuality, creativity, connection, wonder, and joy, Ruth Saxton introduces readers to thirty modern stories featuring "women of a certain age" who prepare for the journey of aging, inhabit the territory, and increasingly become their truest selves.